The Needlepoint ALPHABET Book

The Needlepoint ALPHABET Book

by
MEREDITH & GARY GLADSTONE

WILLIAM MORROW & COMPANY, INC.
NEW YORK

Printed in the United States of America.

Designed by Marion Krupp/Craven & Evans, Creative Graphics

1   2   3   4   5   77   76   75   74   73

Library of Congress Cataloging in Publication Data

Gladstone, Meredith.
  The needlepoint alphabet book.

  1. Canvas embroidery. 2. Alphabets. I. Gladstone, Gary, joint author. II. Title.

TT778.C3G55   746.4′4   73–10028

ISBN 0-688-00197-1

ACKNOWLEDGMENTS

The authors wish to acknowledge with deep appreciation the following people, whose enormous talents combined to help bring this book out of discussion and into print.

Aiko Abe
George Cassa
Narcisse Chamberlain
Pat DeWeese
Julie Fallowfield

CONTENTS

List of
Color Pictures

The Needlepoint ALPHABET Book

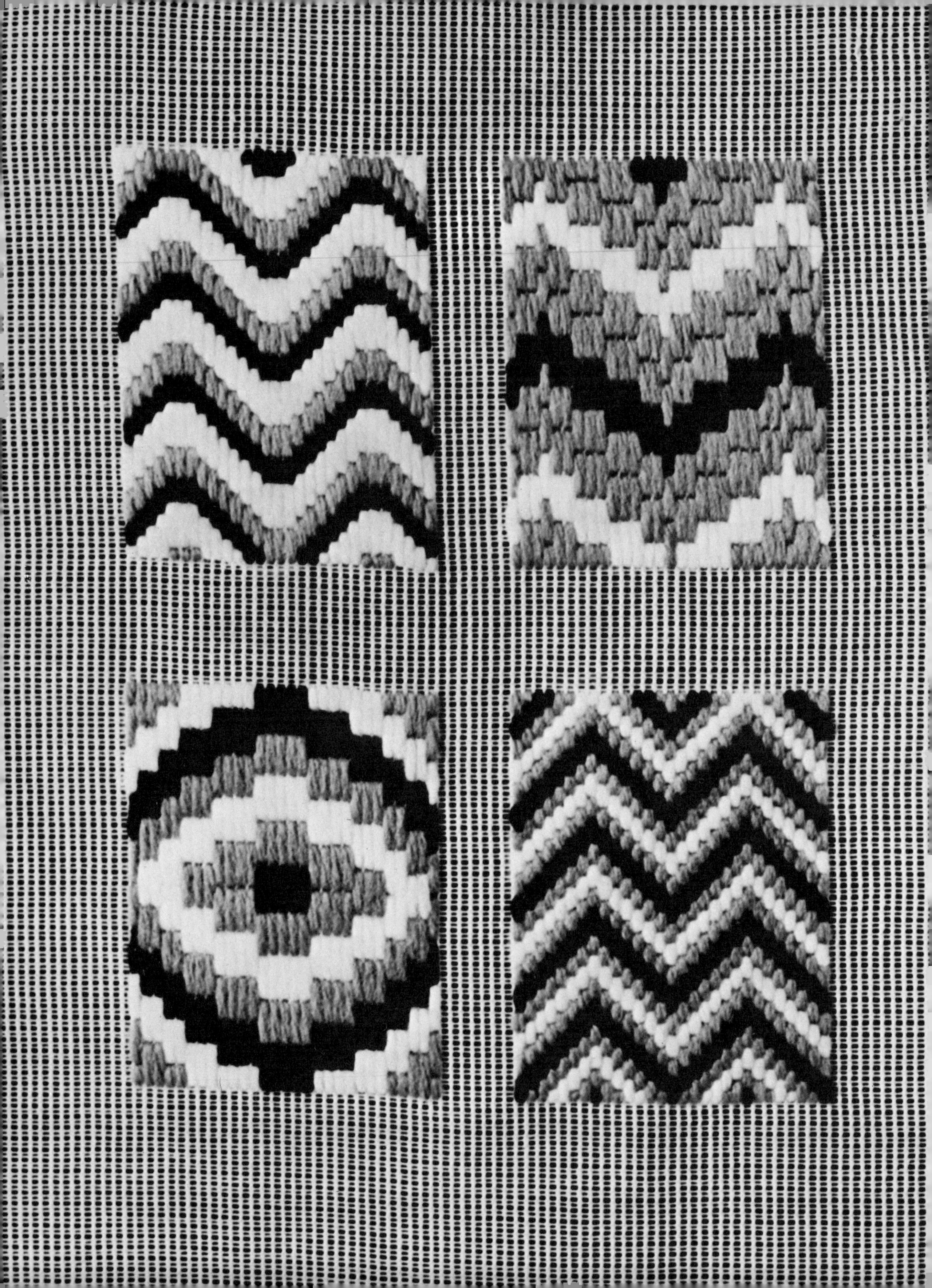

Introduction

Needlepoint has made a special place for itself in today's handcraft revival for many reasons—among them its portability, the beautiful wool colors that have become available, the textures that can be achieved. But, we think, its tremendous popularity is due most of all to the "new" discovery that needlepoint adapts to an endless variety of design ideas.

Grandma's fusty flowered chair-seat covers are no longer the standard image of the appropriate needlepoint design—and the very idea that any particular style of design is the "appropriate" one has disappeared. Instead, an unprecedented number of people with all sorts of different tastes have discovered that needlepoint canvas is a perfect place to create something that expresses their individual ideas. The fact is that needlepoint is by nature such a flexible medium that this new discovery is just a rediscovery of what was true all along. What is new in needlepoint today are the kinds and styles of modern ideas being designed by professionals and by so many people who just love to do needlepoint.

This book is about two things: our own style of design—a modern mixture of colors and graphics; and techniques for getting one's own design onto canvas. Instructions are given in great detail for each of our projects, so they certainly may be copied directly from the book, but the real point of these detailed instructions is to demonstrate *how* we arrived at our designs —and, therefore, how you can arrive at designs that *you* want.

Because Meredith Gladstone is by profession a fashion designer, some of her needlepoint is designed to be worn—belts and hats, ornamental patches that can be sewn on almost anything, including parkas, jeans, robes, blazers, and children's clothing. Other designs are for the house—decorative boxes, pillows, tabletops, album covers, a rug. Every technique needed to finish these articles completely yourself is explained.

Gary Gladstone is a professional photographer and graphic designer. His important contribution to the book is the much overlooked area of idea recognition—or, *How to force yourself to have an idea* (it *can* be done) by establishing an inspiration file of graphic materials collected from everyday 13

14 surroundings. In the chapter "Ideas & Inspiration," he explains how professionals use this system to capture ideas and store them for future use and how needlepointers can use the same system for finding and using fresh, unusual design motifs that truly reflect their own taste.

And, this is the first needlepoint book ever to concentrate on the wealth of design ideas to be found in typography and alphabets. That is why it is called *The Needlepoint Alphabet Book,* and we hope that for this element alone it will prove to be an idea-and-inspiration file in itself.

MEREDITH and GARY GLADSTONE

Ideas & Inspiration

In a clothing store we overheard an incident which really drove home a point about trusting one's own taste. A man was trying on topcoats. Every time he slipped into one, he would shout across the store to his friend, "Hey, Harry, whaddya think of this one? Do you like it? How does it look to you? You think it's good-looking?"

Harry, preoccupied somewhat at the cufflink counter, responded with a dispassionate "Yeah, yeah. It's okay, I guess."

Moments later, the coat customer was in a different coat and again shouting for approval. "Hey, Harry! How about this one? Do you think it's too way-out? Whaddya think, Harry, is it nice?"

Harry was obviously getting annoyed with the repeated invasions of his thoughts and shouted back, "Yeah, yeah, it's okay. I wouldn't buy it, but if you like it, *buy* it. What difference does it make if I like it or not? It's your money. You're going to wear it. If you can't bring your own mind with you shopping, next time bring your wife, not me!"

The coat customer was asking Harry for more than a simple opinion. He was asking poor old Harry to tell him what his own tastes were—something neither Harry nor anyone else could know better than he. And yet, often what *we* like is the one thing we have the most difficulty identifying for ourselves. This holds especially true for tastes in color and design. A shoe salesman can't sell a pair of shoes that pinch, but he can often sell a shoe of a fashionable color that is all wrong for the customer's purpose. Many people sit back and let a total stranger tell them what upholstery fabric or wallpaper pattern they should have, even though he knows nothing about them.

There is a gut feeling we have that we usually overlook. This feeling is one that immediately says *No!* or *Yes!* and it is this primary reaction that is closest to our true tastes. It is a reaction that we often ignore—at best in pursuit of an open-minded policy, or at the worst out of apprehension over what we "ought" to like. It is most important when we sit down to design something to understand gut reactions and to follow them.

When you decide to create something, no one else's opinion should rule your direction. Ask for approval, if you want, but not direction. It's *your* personal work of art.

15

for at least forty years, and we've all seen it so many times that we *don't* see it anymore. But it made a great border for a piece of needlepoint.

Your local printer may have something that should be of great help and that interests us particularly. It is called a specimen sheet, or book. Many printers or typesetting houses offer fairly elaborate collections of the alphabets they feature. These alphabets usually are complete from A to Z and the numerals 0 through 9. There are so many different styles of letters, some highly ornamental, that they are bound to help trigger ideas in making designs out of typefaces. Most specimen books have a section in the back devoted to symbols and borders. This is where you will find a gold mine of graphic devices such as stars, asterisks, pointing fingers, and arrows, along with many very interesting borders that can be lifted directly from the book. Usually there is no charge for these specimen books, and sometimes they are quite elaborate. Try the library, or bookstores, or the book department of an art-supply store. The subjects to check under are Typography, Graphic Arts, or Lettering.

And, in the alphabet chapter of this book are printed some great old and ornate alphabets that can be blown up by photostating and used in many ways.

STEALING WITH A CAMERA

This can be a fabulous way to collect items for your clip file. It's a way to bring things down to manageable size. Imagine that you are passing that old circus poster with a picture of a tiger leaping through a ring of fire. It strikes you as a fun idea for a needlepoint canvas. Shoot it. Getting it onto canvas later is a simple proposition (see page 28). We found a delightful, simple letter "g" in a store window. We photographed it on slide film, then projected it onto canvas, and made a pillow design of one giant "g." Photograph your house and photo-project it onto canvas for tracing.

If not you but someone else in the family is a camera buff or photographer, tell him you'll immortalize his pictures by "publishing" them on canvas. This is a proven recruitment technique, as I can testify, having provided innumerable photographs after just such suggestions from my wife and coauthor of this book.

"g" for Gregory; see photographic transfer, page 28. Rainbow file-card box. Directions for covered boxes, page 149

Materials & Tools

CANVAS

Canvas is the fabric that you start with. It is stiffened with sizing for body and stitching ease. It is woven, usually of cotton, like any fabric with a warp (vertical) and fill (horizontal) thread. Needlepoint canvas, however, is woven in a way that leaves spaces between the threads. You, in turn, make your own finished fabric over the canvas by filling in or covering all the spaces.

There are two basic types of canvas available. *Mono* canvas is canvas with single vertical threads and single horizontal threads forming the fabric. It looks like screening. It generally comes in white and there are many different mesh sizes, from ten threads to the inch to 40 threads to the inch. Mono canvas is fine for pillows, but for other projects I prefer to use penelope canvas, especially for anything that requires a finished edge.

PENELOPE canvas is woven with pairs of vertical threads and pairs of horizontal threads. It generally comes in a natural linen color, but can be found in white. Different sizes are also available—from 15 mesh per inch up to 3½ mesh per inch (which is generally used for rugs). Ten mesh per inch is the most commonly used. Penelope, or double, canvas has an advantage in that the pairs of threads can be split to make smaller squares, so that you can combine petit point with needlepoint on one canvas. I have found that penelope canvas is sturdier and that work on it comes out more neatly. For any project that requires a finished edge (like a box or a luggage tag), double canvas is *essential,* because mono canvas splits and falls apart at the edges.

All canvas, both mono and penelope, is measured by the number of mesh, or threads, per inch. Ten mesh per inch means that there are 10 single threads or 10 pairs of threads for each inch across the canvas the same up and down the canvas—or, 100 stitches per square inch. I usually refer to it as 10/in. canvas. If the canvas is 5 mesh per inch (5/in. canvas), there are

Three types of canvas: 10/in. mono;
10/in. penelope; 5/in. penelope

only 25 stitches per square inch; thus, your work goes much faster and you see results quickly. The higher count the mesh is, the longer it takes to work. However, the higher count enables you to put much finer detail on your canvas. Decide first the kind of design you wish to do and then select the mesh size of canvas that would make your design most effective. Because I like fast results, I often use ten-to-the-inch or five-to-the-inch penelope canvas and split the threads where I want more detail.

Canvas is sometimes available in yarn shops and the needlework departments of department stores, and sometimes not. I find it easier and less frustrating to send away for my canvas from one of the supply houses that advertise in handcraft magazines. It is generally cheaper than in shops, they have a wider variety available, and they deliver fairly quickly.*

The better-quality canvas has a slightly glossy look. Glossy-finish canvas generally is the strongest and can take the most abuse.

YARN

The most important point in your selection of yarn is that it should cover the canvas completely, be bulky enough not to leave gaps or spaces, and be able to withstand any abuse. For a chair seat, very durable long-staple yarn such as tapestry or Persian wool should be used, whereas for a picture to be framed, anything goes. The mesh size of your canvas determines the thickness of yarn to use. The more mesh per inch, the finer the yarn; and the fewer mesh per inch, the thicker the yarn. Always try out the yarn on a small section of your canvas so that you can see how it will look.

Needlepoint wools such as the tapestry or Persian have a long, smooth fiber, while knitting yarn has a shorter fiber. A longer fiber is generally tougher and will be less likely to pull and snag while being worked. The following are some of the yarns you may use for various purposes:

CREWEL WOOL is a two-ply yarn that is generally sold in 20- to 25-yard skeins. This type of yarn covers 14/in. canvas or smaller and is very good for petit point. It comes in a good range of colors and is also used for crewel embroidery.

PERSIAN WOOL is also a two-ply wool that is sold in three-thread strands. As it comes, it is perfect for 10/in. canvas, but the threads can be separated and used for finer work. There is a good color selection and it is sold by the ounce, so you can buy small quantities.

TAPESTRY WOOL is a four-ply yarn that comes in approximately 40-yard skeins—or in approximately 9-yard skeins to use for small areas of color. It covers 10/in. or 12/in. canvas, is available in matched dye lots, and is mothproofed (as are most wool yarns). The color ranges are good, although very bright colors are sometimes hard to find in tapestry yarn.

KNITTING WORSTED is a four-ply wool yarn which is often good for 10/in. canvas. This type of yarn cannot be separated, so it is only good

---

* The following mail-order houses can supply catalogs: *Merribee,* 2904 West Lancaster, P. O. Box 9680, Fort Worth, Texas 76107; The *Stitchery,* 204 Worcester Turnpike, Wellesley Hills, Massachusetts 02181.

for the one size of canvas it happens to cover well. It comes in 4-ounce or 2-ounce skeins and the color selection is limited, although I have found some of the best bright colors in this yarn.

RUG YARN is a three-ply wool that has a rough texture and is good for 8/in. or lower canvas. It generally comes in 22-yard skeins. There is a smaller selection of colors in rug yarn because it is not as widely used as needlepoint yarn. In some instances, I have used instead three or four strands of knitting worsted at once on large canvas.

NOVELTY YARNS such as silk, cotton, blends, and metallics can be used in combination with regular yarns to achieve unusual effects. Any sort of yarn that looks interesting should be tried. Just remember always to experiment first on a small area of the canvas.

I use all types of yarn for my work and always like to have a good supply around. Whenever I see a color that I like, or a texture I would like to try, I buy it and file it away. I use plastic bags and fill each bag with shades of one color; all shades of red in one, shades of blue in another, etc. The small bags are put in a large canvas tote and stored in the closet. Bags that sweaters are sold in are ideal for your yarn supplies, especially the ones with snap or zipper tops.

AMOUNTS OF YARN USED. Once you have decided which yarn you like, work a 1-inch square in the stitch you intend to use and note the amount of yarn used. Figure the number of square inches to be covered by each color, and multiply this by the amount used to work one inch. This will give you the approximate yarn yardage for your project. To figure the number of skeins, divide your yardage by the number of yards indicated on the skein wrapper. When in doubt, always buy more than you think you need, so you don't run short—especially for a background color, because it may be impossible to match your color exactly later on.

NEEDLES

Needlepoint needles are called tapestry needles and have long eyes and blunt points. The higher the number of the needle, the smaller the mesh on which it can be used. Lower needle numbers are used on larger mesh. You can determine which size you like best by trying several sizes from the chart below and deciding which one threads the easiest and goes through the canvas with the least resistance. Good needles are steel, and when they don't slide easily they need to be sharpened or smoothed. Do this by running the needle through an emery bag.

GUIDE FOR NEEDLES

Canvas Size	Needle Size
3½, 5 inch	#13 or large-eyed rug needle
7, 8 inch	#15
10, 12, 14 inch	#17 or 18
16, 18 inch	#19 or 20
Petit-point or fine canvas	#21 to 24

THIMBLE

When I started doing needlepoint, I couldn't use a thimble because it seemed very awkward and tended to slow down my work. After a few weeks, my finger became so tender I could hardly push the needle. I tried wrapping the finger with a Band-Aid because it was much less awkward than a thimble and seemed to provide a little insulation. But the needle just chewed up the Band-Aid and the sticky adhesive was always pulling bits of yarn in all directions.

That's when I rediscovered the thimble. Now I can't even sew on a button without using a thimble. It's become a part of my anatomy. Thimbles come in different sizes. Slip one on and wiggle your finger. The proper size should just barely stay on. Too snug a fit, and your finger will be throbbing in twenty minutes.

SCISSORS

A small pair of good-quality, sharp, pointed scissors is essential. I use a fold-up type that is ideal for carrying around. Canvas cutting should be done with a longer pair of desk scissors.

I find it easiest to keep my scissors, thimble, and needles all together in a kit. Perhaps your first project can be your own personalized needlepoint tool kit, which is the first project described later on.

TECHNIQUES

Techniques

Whenever you start a project, you begin by choosing the type of canvas for what you want to make and deciding how large or small the piece needs to be. Cut a piece of canvas that allows at least 3 to 4 inches, or more, all around than the outline of your project. Most of the projects in this book are done on 10-mesh-per-inch or 5-mesh-per-inch canvas. If you want a project that will work up quickly, use large canvas, 3½ to 5 mesh per inch. You cannot get small detail on it, but for projects such as rugs it goes quickly. I like to work on 10-mesh-per-inch canvas because you can get some detail on it and it is not too trying on the eyes. For finer detail, use canvas 12, 14, or 18 mesh per inch. If you think you just might play around with adding a border motif or more background to your original design, allow plenty of extra canvas on all four sides. You should always cut in a straight line between two threads of the canvas.

Remember when marking your design on canvas that the warp threads —those parallel to the selvage, or edge of the uncut canvas—should always run up and down. These are the same as the straight grain on a piece of fabric and there is less stretching in this direction. On penelope or double canvas this is easy to keep track of, as the pairs of threads running visibly closest together are the warp threads. On mono or single canvas, this warp is not easy to see if the selvage is cut away. So mark the top of the canvas before you cut it so you don't forget which direction is up and down.

When you have cut your canvas to the size you want, there will be raw edges. These pointy edges fray. They split and snag your yarn and slow down your stitching. The best and easiest way to prevent this is to bind them with masking tape. It comes in different widths, the best being ¾" or 1" for 10/in. canvas (or for any mesh smaller than that) and tape 2" wide for 5/in. canvas or larger.

To apply the tape to the canvas, cut a length of tape for one side and lay it on a flat surface with the sticky side up. Now place the canvas on the tape, covering half the width of the tape. Rub it lightly so it will be sure to stick. Now fold the remaining half of the tape to the front and press it down. Do this on all sides, then run the taped edges between your fingers, using some pressure to make them secure.

27

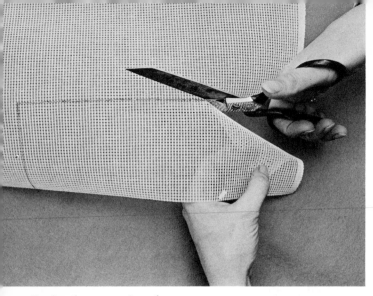

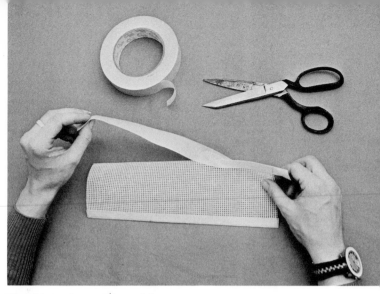

Cutting between threads   Finishing edges with masking tape

Make a note of the overall measurements of the taped canvas and draw this area, perfectly squared out, on a piece of brown paper. (Use a *waterproof* marking pen, because you will use this paper later as a guide for blocking once your work is completed.)

Tracing a Design Onto Canvas

Many designs can be sketched directly onto the canvas by placing the canvas over the design and tracing it. Or, if you can't see the design well enough through the canvas, make a bold black-line tracing of it on tracing paper and then retrace from that onto the canvas. I usually use the tracing technique (rather than graphing, described later) for free-form types of design—drawings of flowers, or copies of fabric designs, or anything that is not geometric. On page 44 is a photograph of the best way to pin the canvas over the design —with pushpins in the four corners of the paper underneath.

If you find a design you like but which is not the right size, you can take it to a photostat company (look in the Yellow Pages under "Photo Copying"). Tell them the size you want, either larger or smaller; specify the exact dimensions you want the final design to be.

Once you have the photostat, place your canvas over it and use a *waterproof* marking pen to trace the design onto the canvas. You can use colored waterproof marking pens to outline color areas if you want. Be sure you buy the colors in waterproof pens only, so that when you block your canvas they do not bleed through and discolor your yarn.

You can also color the entire canvas. If your original design is in color, you can place the canvas over the design and paint in the colors, using either waterproof marking pens or acrylic paints that are insoluble in water after drying. Let the canvas dry thoroughly before starting to stitch on it.

Photographic Transfer & Using a Projector

There are two ways to use photography to get designs onto canvas. One is to shoot the subject with film that will provide a print (including Polaroid). Then the print is used to refer to when you make a freehand drawing to trace onto canvas, or is graphed and redrawn on canvas (see "Free-hand Graphing").

The other method is our favorite. Almost anything is possible with it. What you do is first photograph the subject with a film that will provide slides.

Place the slide in a projector aimed at a blank wall space. Put a piece of canvas on the wall and hold it in place with masking tape. Now turn the projector on and move the projector back and forth until the image falling on the canvas is the size you want. (A projector equipped with a zoom lens will make sizing of the image easier, because it won't be necessary to move the projector itself so much in order to cover the canvas with the image you've selected.)

Focus the lens so that the picture on the canvas is sharp. With the projector on, trace the outlines of the image with a waterproof marking pen. (It is wise to put a piece of nonporous material, such as waxed paper or aluminum foil, between the canvas and the wall so that the marker won't mar the wall.) You may find it easier to project the image onto brown wrapping paper rather than canvas and draw the image on the paper. The paper can then be placed on a more convenient work surface, a table, with the canvas placed over it, and then you can redraw the image onto the canvas.

Have the local photo shop send the slide out to have a print made from it. The print, which will cost about forty cents, will serve as a handy color guide, easier to use than a slide, which you have to hold up to a light and squint at to see.

Some museums will permit visitors to take pictures of the art displayed. This can provide you with a great chance to use the photo-transfer technique to design a canvas from your favorite work of art. In many cases, museums sell high-quality slides of their collection as well as of great works from museums around the world. Many public libraries maintain files of slides that are available for borrowing.

If you don't own a projector, most photo-equipment shops will rent one on a daily basis. If you do rent, specify a zoom lens. If you have access to a photo darkroom, a photographic enlarger is also an excellent tool for projecting an image to be traced. Simply substitute the slide for a negative, turn out the lights, and you're ready to trace.

Shooting letters from the street

Photo projection on the wall

Tracing around the letter

Print of original slide and needlepoint in progress

The traced letter

It is possible to make color-copy slides of material in a book, using a reflex type of camera. Simply prop the book up near a light or, preferably, out in the sun, and, if necessary, use a close-up attachment to photograph the picture you wish to project on canvas. Often photo shops can provide this service for you. If yours doesn't, check the Yellow Pages under "Slides and Film Strips" or "Photographers—Commercial."

On a large project such as a rug, it is considerably less expensive to make a slide and, if necessary, rent a projector than to pay for a series of oversize photostats.

Graphs

A musical score is a composer's graph of his musical ideas. The score is a specific indication of what note is to be played at what time and in what manner. If the musician reads his score correctly, the final result is an accurate reconstruction of the composer's music.

In needlepoint, the score for the graphic idea can be conveyed stitch by stitch on graph paper. Followed carefully, a graph leads to a precise rendering of the original idea on finished canvas. And after learning to read a graph, it is easy to understand how to make your own. This skill makes it possible to test ideas before committing them to canvas. Making changes and corrections with pencil and paper is a lot easier than revising stitches already taken on canvas.

READING A GRAPH

One *square* on the graph paper equals one *stitch* on the canvas. As an example of this, we shall graph out a word on paper and then show it finished on canvas. Try this yourself.

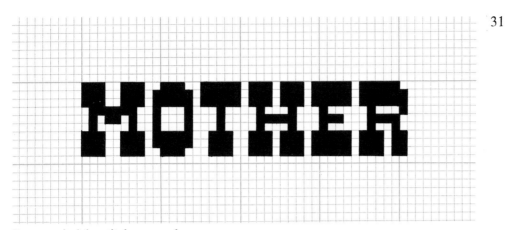

Letters stitch by stitch on graph paper

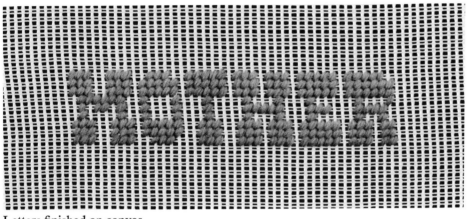

Letters finished on canvas

CENTERING

Whenever you want to make a design that is symmetrical or exactly centered within a given space, graphing is the best technique to use because it's all very mathematical (well, simple arithmetic is all it is), and you can get a design to come out perfectly. It's also very interesting to experiment with designs on graph paper to see just what you yourself can come up with. Then, if you like what you've done, the squares of the graph paper tell you how to do it over in needlepoint stitches and also how to place it on your canvas so it will be properly centered.

As an example, we shall set up the problem of putting the letter G in the center of a patch of a particular size. First, decide what size patch it is you want to make, and then draw the outline on the canvas lightly with a pale-blue drawing pencil.

Now count the number of vertical threads you have for the total width of the patch and divide this by two. For instance, I have 45 vertical threads, so 45 divided by two equals 22½. Therefore, thread Number 23 is the center line (or, 22 + 1 + 22 = 45). Mark the thread the length of the patch with your pencil.

If the number were an even number—say, 46—you would have *two* center threads (or, 22 + 1 + 1 + 22 = 46). Mark the canvas on either side of the two threads with the pencil.

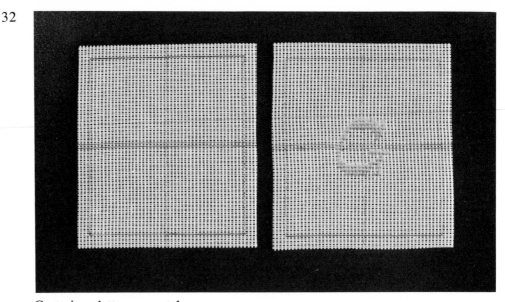

Centering a letter on a patch

Count out the patch on the canvas the other way, horizontally, and find the horizontal center thread—or threads—by the same procedure. Where your lines cross will be the center. The patch shown in two stages in the photograph is 45 threads wide by 50 threads long with the G centered on the crossed lines.

Decide where—at what particular stitch—it will be most convenient to start working the letter. Count out the location of that stitch, using the center lines as reference points, and mark it on the canvas. Now you can work the G following the placement of stitches shown on one of the alphabet graphs. Your design will come out centered on the patch.

MAKING YOUR OWN GRAPH

When you want the details of a design to be absolutely accurate, symmetrical, or geometric, it is best to lay it all out on graph paper first so that it will be mathematically exact. Any design can be graphed but it does take some patience, so I use this technique mainly for geometric patterns or repeat patterns. For instance, for a bandana-scarf pattern, in which the four quarters of the design are identical, graphing is ideal.

Small pads of graph paper for small designs are easy to find in any stationery store. If you want to do a large design, you will need large sheets from an art-supply or draftsman's-supply store. Some large sheets are sold in pads, others as separate sheets. If you need a sheet larger than what is locally available, simply paste or tape sections of graph paper together, using Scotch Magic tape. It is transparent and can be drawn over. Be sure to match the graphed lines exactly where you join the paper. Buy the paper graphed with the same scale grid as the canvas mesh size (10 sq. per inch, 5 sq. per inch, etc.) you wish to use.

Decide what you want to graph. I shall take a bandana with a symmetrical center motif as an example. I want to make all four quarters come

out the same. With masking tape, tape the scarf, evenly stretched, to a window. Mark it into quarters by drawing a vertical and a horizontal center line
on it with dressmaker's chalk. Now tape the graph paper on top of the upper
right-hand quarter of the scarf, with the lower left-hand corner of the graph
paper exactly at the center of the scarf and the left side and bottom of the
paper lined up with the center lines that are drawn on the scarf. Trace only
this quarter of the design on the graph paper. You now have a rough line
drawing. Put the paper on a table and work the rough design into a careful
graph by outlining the squares that are closest to the lines of the design.

Start transferring your design to canvas by reading from the graph
for the upper right-hand quarter section first. Then turn your *graph* (not
the canvas!) one quarter turn to do an adjoining quarter. Turn it another
quarter turn each time you start a new section. All you are doing is reading
exactly the same graph from four different directions, with the "center corner"
of the graph always pointing to the center of the design that is growing on
the canvas. The finished canvas will be symmetrical no matter which way you
turn it.

Tracing a scarf pattern   Graphing the traced lines

Note that there is such a thing as tracing-paper graph paper. With
that you do not need to tape the original design to a window to see it through
the paper. Or, some designs are bold enough to see adequately for tracing
through regular graph paper.

FREE-HAND GRAPHING

It is possible to change the size of a small or large design by drawing
a rough graph in pencil or pen directly on the subject selected. (If it cannot
be defaced by pencil or pen lines, trace it onto tracing paper and draw your
graph lines on that.)

Drawing a graph free-hand

Suppose you see a letter in a newspaper advertisement that would make a nice initial for a patch. It is, however, too small and must be enlarged to be usable, let's say up to four inches. Using a ruler, make five equally spaced vertical lines over the design, then five horizontal ones. What you have created is a graph which can now be upgraded by free-hand drawing onto regular graph paper that you have blocked out in squares four times as large. You use the squares on your original newspaper initial as reference points for where to draw the curves and straight lines of the initial onto your enlarged graph. You can do the same thing backward to make a subject smaller.

Either of these graphs could have been the "original," depending on whether you were enlarging or reducing the design.

Stitches

Stitches are to needlepoint what the strokes of brushes or palette knives are to painting. The painter will select a brush or knife and make a particular stroke to create texture and suggest a mood. Stitches help express mood and are directly responsible for the texture of needlepoint. To have a good repertoire of stitches is almost as important as having a good collection of wool colors in helping to present your ideas on canvas. There are stitches that suggest fire or waves; others have the solid look of a brick wall. Some are as delicate as fine miniature mosaic. Combinations of stitches can create complicated textures that are very enjoyable. Stitches, like brush strokes and paint colors, can help impart an emotional quality to your work. The bargello is bold, energetic, exciting, while the continental is sedate, quiet, neat and polite.

There are a few basic needlepoint stitches to learn in order to do any type of needlepoint design and many variations on those basic stitches. But always, your purpose is to cover the entire canvas with stitches of yarn, and any yarn you use should do just that—*cover* the canvas. Whether you use an established stitch or invent your own, just remember that the mesh of the canvas should never show through on the front. If the stitch you choose is not covering the canvas, then the yarn size is wrong and you should add another strand of it or use a heavier yarn. Before starting a project, always do some practice stitching to be sure you will be using the right weight of wool

Initial patch, "finished clean"; see page 45

38   The canvas can be covered with slanting stitches (always slanting to the right), vertical stitches, or horizontal stitches. There are many variations on the basic ones and many different stitches can be combined on one canvas.

Slanted Stitches

THE HALF-CROSS STITCH

There are three ways of producing the basic slanted needlepoint stitch. The most commonly known has long been the half-cross stitch. It is done from left to right, one horizontal row at a time. When you get to the end of one row, you turn the canvas upside down and continue working again from left to right. This works on penelope canvas because the double mesh holds the yarn, but it is not good for mono canvas. Always remember that this and all slanted stitches on your finished canvas should look the same on the front and should slant in the same direction, i.e., from lower left to upper right.

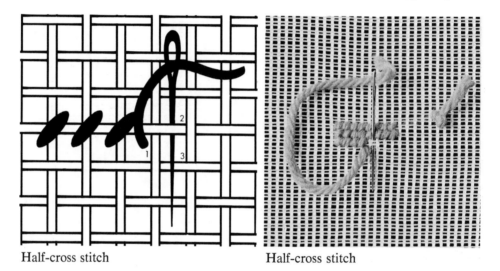

Half-cross stitch   Half-cross stitch

The half-cross stitch will not take much wear and tear because there is not much backing of yarn on the reverse side, so it is not advisable for a seat cover or anything that might take hard use. Also, I rarely use it because the stitches are not even enough and because the canvas gets very distorted and is difficult to block back into shape.

The chief advantage of the half-cross stitch is that it takes the least amount of yarn to cover the canvas. About ¾ yard of yarn will cover a square inch on 10/in. canvas (a space 10 mesh across and 10 mesh up and down).

THE CONTINENTAL STITCH (OR TENT STITCH)

The continental stitch looks the same as the half-cross on the front of the canvas but provides good backing, so it can be used for projects that will take some wear. This stitch is worked from right to left (the opposite of the half-cross) and as you reach the end of a row, the canvas is turned upside down, just as for the half-cross. Because the stitch is worked from right to

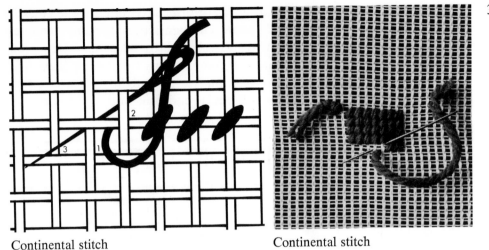

Continental stitch   Continental stitch

left, the yarn is carried under each stitch on the back and the finished piece has a double thickness of wool. The canvas becomes distorted if the continental stitch is used over a large area, as it does pull the canvas out of shape and also makes blocking difficult. But the stitch is a good one for a row of outline or any tiny area of color and is often used in combination with the basketweave when there are many small bits of color in a pattern.

The continental takes about 1 yard of wool to cover a square inch on 10/in. canvas.

THE BASKETWEAVE STITCH (OR DIAGONAL TENT STITCH)

The basketweave stitch is so named because of the woven look of the pattern that is formed on the back of the work. It is the most durable of all the basic stitches and produces the neatest and most even work. Because it has both horizontal and vertical tension, it does not distort the canvas. It is worked from the upper right-hand corner of the canvas and fills it up with diagonal rows of stitches that accumulate toward the lower left. You do not have to turn the canvas when using the basketweave stitch and can keep the design right side up all the time. Use this stitch even on tiny areas if you can, but the continental stitch is the alternate one to use when the basketweave is not convenient in small areas.

Make sure when you start a new piece of yarn to continue the row of basketweave in the proper direction, because there will be a faint diagonal ridge showing on the front if you don't. If you stop in the middle of a row, be sure when you start again to continue in the same direction. If you stop at the end of a row, you must remember to start the next row at the *same* end. One way to remember where to begin: When you tie off the yarn, instead of also cutting off the tail of it on the back, pull it through to the front at the point where you must start again. It will remind you where to start days or months later. (It should be trimmed off, of course, before you start to stitch again.)

It takes about 1 yard of yarn to fill a square inch on 10/in. canvas with basketweave.

40   The three basic slanted stitches, as described, cover only one crossed mesh of the canvas, but you can do many variations covering more than one. These long stitches are laid on the canvas in geometrical patterns. You can experiment with your own patterns and combinations by drawing them first on graph paper. Remember not to pull the yarn too tightly when covering more than one mesh, or the canvas will buckle and your work will be uneven.

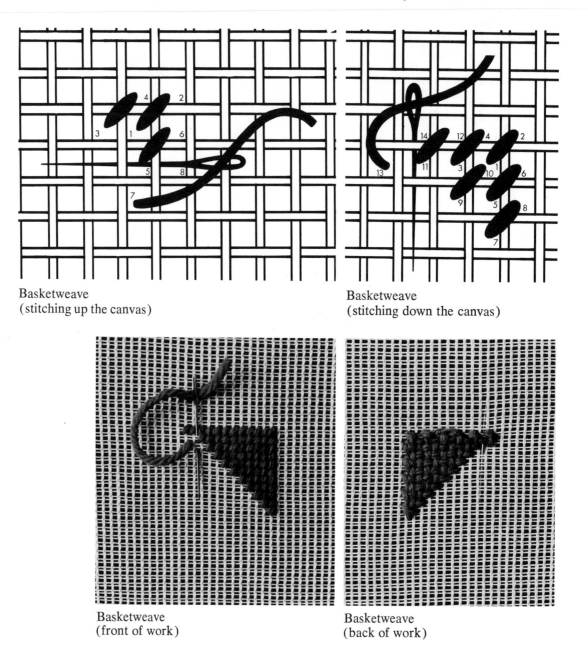

Basketweave
(stitching up the canvas)

Basketweave
(stitching down the canvas)

Basketweave
(front of work)

Basketweave
(back of work)

THE MOSAIC STITCH (SLANTED GEOMETRIC)

The mosaic stitch is a good example of the idea of slanted-stitch variations, from which you can derive many more stitches.

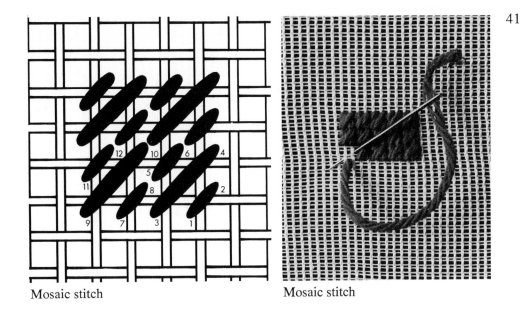

Mosaic stitch

Mosaic stitch

THE GOBELIN STITCH (VERTICAL STITCH)

Straight Stitches

This is the basic stitch for working yarn vertically over the canvas mesh rather than slanting it. You can cover one, two, three, or four horizontal canvas threads at a time. When using this stitch, your yarn should be relatively thick to cover the canvas. So once again, test the yarn on a corner of the canvas. Because you're covering more than one thread at a time, your work will go fast. This is a good stitch to use when you have a large background to do.

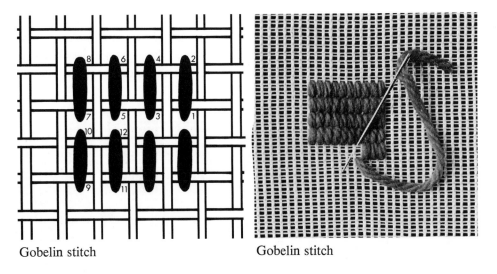

Gobelin stitch

Gobelin stitch

THE BRICK STITCH

The brick stitch is a variation of the straight gobelin stitch. The basic principle is the same as for the bargello stitch (described next). It is worked

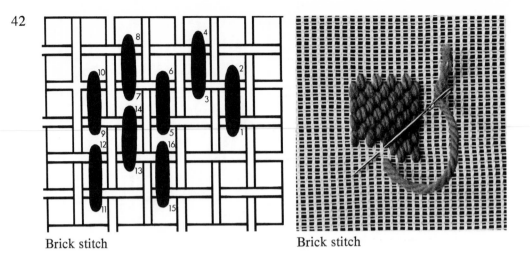

Brick stitch   Brick stitch

across the canvas in slanting rows and when completed has the look of a neatly laid brick wall. I especially like the brick stitch for backgrounds because it works up quickly and has an interesting texture. Your yarn should, again, be quite thick for this stitch so canvas will not show through. Work from right to left, then from left to right on the next row. You do not have to turn the canvas.

THE BARGELLO STITCH (FLAME STITCH)

The bargello stitch is basically the straight gobelin stitch and also a variation of the brick stitch, done in different yarn colors to get zigzag patterns that look like flames. Bargello covers 2 to 8 horizontal mesh of the canvas and the variations are very numerous. The patterns you produce depend on the number of threads the stitches cover, the number of steps up and down, and the points at which these changes are made. If you are making each "flame" a different color, you can start each color at the right and work across to the left, or you can work back and forth all in the same color, as shown in the diagram.

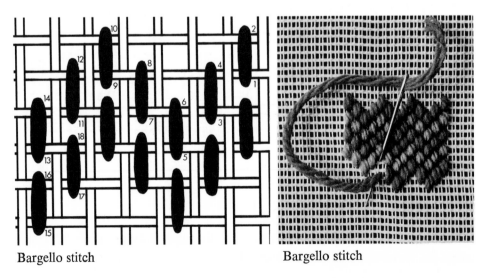

Bargello stitch   Bargello stitch

HORIZONTAL VARIATIONS ON STRAIGHT STITCHES

All of the vertical stitches, including the bargello, can be done horizontally instead. The stitches are the same but are taken across the vertical threads of the canvas. (The vertical stitches were taken up and down across the horizontal threads.) Try combining vertical and horizontal stitches on the same canvas.

Combined horizontal and vertical stitches   Bargello variations

Blocking

Once your work is completed, it will have become distorted—somewhat diamond-shaped rather than squared off—because of the pulling and tugging of stitches. Before it can be framed or made into a pillow or whatever, the stitched canvas must be blocked to return it to its original shape.

Take the piece of paper on which you originally marked the outline of the overall canvas and tack the paper to a piece of board (soft fiberboard works best) or other flat surface. Or transfer the outline directly to the board, making sure that the corners are at right angles and that your measurements exactly duplicate the original sketch. Always use *waterproof* marking pens when marking board or paper. Otherwise, the steaming during blocking will cause ink to transfer to the needlepoint.

44   You will need pins to hold the canvas, and the best kind are the non-rusting long T-pins. I find that wig pins bought in any dime store serve very well on fiberboard, too. They are long enough and have flat heads so they can be easily pushed in and pulled out. Buy too many rather than just enough Skimping with pins during blocking will prove extremely frustrating.

Take your canvas and dampen the back of it with a wet sponge. It should not be soaked through but should be damp enough to feel slightly limp. Place the canvas face down on the drawn outline. Push in a T-pin at each corner of the canvas. The pins should go in at about a 45° angle, leaning away from the center of the canvas. Pin the corners first, then the center of each edge, then between the centers, and so on, until there are pins all around, about ½″ to 1″ apart. The canvas will need some tugging and pulling to get it to match the original outlines on the board.

Now take a pressing cloth larger than the finished canvas and wet it thoroughly. Place the wet cloth over the canvas, and with a hot iron press your work until it's fairly dry, but leave the canvas pinned on the board until it has dried completely (at least a day). If the canvas is badly distorted, you may have to block it several times.

If your canvas persists in shrinking back to its distorted shape, it is advisable to apply rabbit-skin glue to the back of it. Do this *after* the canvas has dried, but while it is still pinned square on the board. Rabbit-skin glue is a sizing that will make the needlepoint a little stiff but will guarantee the shape you want. It can be purchased in any art-supply store. Mix it fresh for each project: Mix 1 ounce of the dry glue to 1 cup of water. Let the glue soak until it is soft. Now heat it slowly in a saucepan, stirring constantly, until it is smooth. Let the glue cool and it will become a jell. Spread it thinly on the back of your dry, blocked canvas with a palette knife, butter knife, or spatula. Be sure not to put on so much that it soaks through to the front. Now set your board aside until the canvas has again dried completely.

Dampen the canvas.

Pin the canvas over the original outline.

Press, using a pressing cloth.

There are some things in needlepoint that look much better if the edges are "finished clean." This technique makes your work very neat and not bulky from excess canvas folded back along the finished edge. It is ideal for finishing belts, tabletops, place mats, or patches and pockets for clothes. You finish edges clean after the design on canvas has been totally completed and blocked, and the process works *only on penelope canvas.*

We shall use the edge of a patch (page 35) as our example. You have done the patch completely and blocked it, and want to have neat, flat edges. The first thing to do is to cut off the excess canvas. Trim it off, leaving three rows of double threads all around. Your cutting line is between the third and fourth double threads.

You now have three rows of double-thread lines. Using the *center* pair as your foldline, bend back the canvas, pressing firmly between your fingers. Make sure you do this carefully so that you do not rip any of the threads out.

Trim the edges between the 3rd and 4th threads.

Fold back two threads of canvas.

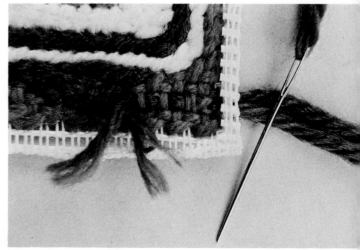

Start the yarn on the back.

Stitch around the work.

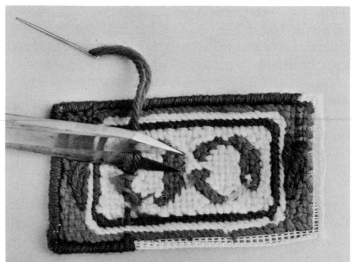

Finish off on the back.

Thread your needle with *double yarn* and run several basting stitches across the back of the canvas to secure the yarn. Now bring the needle up through one of the holes at the edge, then up again through the next hole. The yarn wraps around the edge of the canvas, binding it. Continue all the way around in every hole with this stitch until you have finished the four edges. Make sure you catch all the canvas threads—two sets of double threads in each stitch—so you don't have loose threads showing. When beginning or ending your yarn, run several stitches through the back of your work.

Joining Seams & Making Corners

It is possible to make three-dimensional shapes in needlepoint by joining seams as you would do in sewing any other fabric. You must use penelope canvas, however.

The hat (page 141) is put together by joining two seams at the back. Work your canvas completely, including blocking; the piece should always be blocked flat first, because it is impossible to press after it has been

Start stitch at the corner.

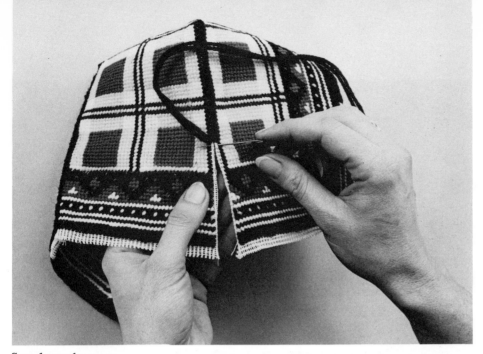

Sew down the seam.

joined. Then trim away excess canvas along the edges to be joined. Leave about four or five rows of double canvas threads. Bring together the trimmed edges and, with your needle coming from the inside, come out at one top hole on the canvas and go across and *down into* the matching top hole on the other side of the hat. Continue this stitch, making sure you match the holes, all the way down to the far end of the seam. Bind off the yarn by running it under several stitches on the back of your needlework.

Backing with Felt

On some projects—for instance, belts—it's nice to have a finished look on the inside as well as on the outside. I find that felt is an excellent backing because you can cut it to the shape you need without having to turn in the edges. It is easily applied with spray adhesive.

Once your project is completely finished, blocked, and finished clean (page 45), pin it, right side up, to a piece of felt, and trace around the object on the felt. Remove the needlepoint.

Trace outline of the needlepoint onto felt.

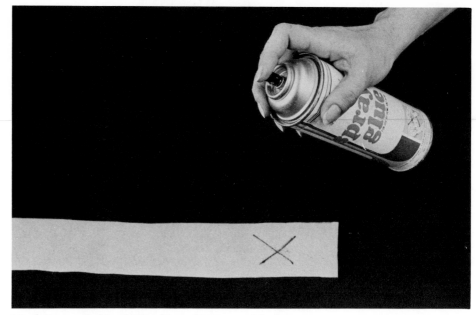

Mark "wrong" side of felt with an X. Spray with glue.

Mark with an X the wrong side of the felt (or the side that is to be glued to the back of the object). Trim away the excess felt by cutting slightly *inside* your tracing lines. Lay the felt with the X side up on a large piece of paper. (This is so you do not spray glue on everything.) Spray the entire surface of the felt with glue, then place it evenly and smoothly on the back of the needlework and let it dry. If any edges of felt show on the right side, trim off the excess with scissors after the piece is dry.

If you prefer, you can also sew the felt by hand to the back of the needlepoint with small hemming stitches along the edges. I prefer the glue because it holds better and gives the finished piece extra body.

Place glued felt on the needlepoint.   Trim any felt that shows on the right side.

Sometime you may want to secure a piece of finished needlework to a hard surface so it will be there permanently. You can use this technique for putting canvas on a box or a book cover or even a tabletop. You will need Elmer's glue and pushpins ½″ to ¾″ long, or T-pins. You will also need your canvas completely blocked to the dimensions of the shape to which it is to be applied.

Glueing Finished Work to Hard Surface

Get a small cup and a small paintbrush about 1″ wide with the bristles cut straight off. Pour some Elmer's glue into the cup and add a few drops of water to thin it. Now paint the glue onto the hard surface. Allow the glue to dry slightly so that it is tacky to the touch.

Now take your finished canvas and place it on the glued surface. Secure the corners first; use pushpins if the surface is wood, or use T-pins if the surface is softer (such as an album or book cover). Put pins all around the edges where you want the needlepoint to hold, and leave them in until the glue is completely dry; it's best to let it dry overnight. Once the glue is dry, you can take the pins out and your canvas should stay on forever.

When the edge of the needlepoint is "finished clean" and is to line up exactly with the edge of the object it is being glued to (such as a tabletop or box), be sure to use plenty of pins to hold it or it may not stick properly. However, when you take the pins out, if the edge is not quite firmly stuck, lift it up, apply more glue with a small brush or a toothpick, then pin the edge down and allow it to dry once again.

Special techniques for applying needlepoint to covered boxes are explained beginning on page 149 and to a book cover beginning on page 167.

To many, the backing for a pillow may appear very difficult when, in fact, it can be done quite easily. You need a piece of fabric about 6″ larger each way than your finished needlepoint, a zipper as long as the width of the needlepoint, and a sewing machine to put it together.

Making a Backing for a Pillow

First, measure your finished and blocked needlepoint and then cut out your fabric, allowing 1″ seam allowance on three sides and 2″ seam allowance on the bottom only. Now measure about 4″ up from the *bottom,* and cut your fabric straight across. This is the seam for setting in your zipper.

Place the zipper right side down on the *right* side of the small piece of fabric you have cut; line the zipper up about 1″ from the top edge of the fabric. Now stitch by machine along the entire length of the zipper, stitching as close to the zipper as you can. Now turn back the zipper, turn under the 1″ seam allowance, and press so the zipper and fabric lie flat.

Now do the same thing along the bottom of the other piece of fabric, making sure you line up the sides of the two pieces. Then fold the top (big) piece of fabric over the zipper so that the zipper is covered, and baste this tuck in place. Press, then stitch the tuck by machine.

Open the zipper slightly so you can turn the "pillowcase" right side out after it has been stitched together. Put the *right sides* of the fabric backing and of the needlepoint together, and baste all around. Then stitch by machine, slightly *inside* the needlepoint so that no canvas will show; stitch on the needlepoint side so you can see what you are doing.

Trim the seams all around so there is ½″ left. Trim the excess fabric in the corners by cutting them off at an angle.

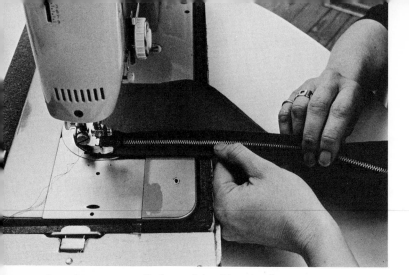

Sew zipper on small piece, right sides together.

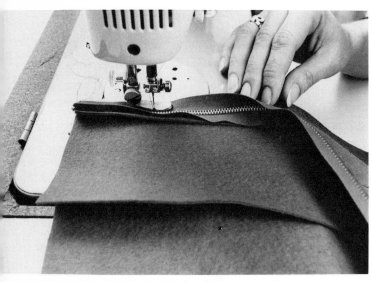

Sew zipper onto large piece, right sides together.

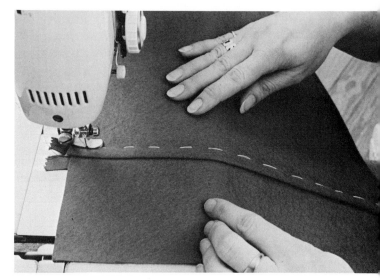

Fold large piece over zipper; baste. Topstitch by machine.

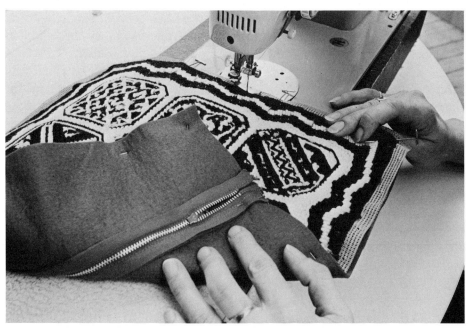

Stitch backing to needlepoint.

Turn pillow casing right side out.

Now slide your zipper open, and turn the pillow inside out. Press the edges lightly on the fabric side, using steam, but do not press flat.

If you do not want to put in a zipper, you can sew around three sides of your pillow. Turn it inside out, put your stuffing in, and then sew the bottom across by hand.

You can buy standard-size stuffed pillows covered with muslin at some stores. If your needlepoint is not a standard size, you should make your own muslin pillow. (*Don't* stuff the needlepoint case.) You can stuff the muslin with kapok or Dacron, which can be bought at almost any department store. You can also stuff it with down, which you can get from an upholsterer. Make the muslin case the same way you do the outside case, but eliminate the zipper: Sew up three sides, turn, stuff, and sew up the fourth side by hand.

Cleaning Your Work

Keeping exposed needlework clean can be a problem. My mother's house has "no-step" and "no-sit" zones all over it. Her favorite needlepoint rug and chair near the fireplace have hardly been used since they were put there. Because it can be difficult to clean needlework, most exposed work must be protected. But it's hard to protect a belt, key tag, hat, patch, book cover, or chair cover from being soiled during normal use. Since washing will cause loss of shape, shrinkage, and possibly running colors, dry cleaning is obviously called for. But how do you dry clean work that is fastened to a chair or bound around a book? Luckily, modern consumerism has brought forth a miracle in a can —the spray spot lifter. Texize K2r is a chemical marketed in most cleaning-goods departments of supermarkets and hardware stores. The product is available in many forms—liquid, gel, and spray can. We recommend the spray can. A mist of cleaning solvent is sprayed directly onto the work. Take care to follow instructions on the can. The solvent dries in about five minutes to

52   a loose, chalky, white powder ready for removal. In drying, it has entrapped dirt particles and emulsified oils. For small pieces, brush the powder away with a clothes brush or the brush-topped K2r can. An amazing amount of grime will be removed from the needlework. For larger areas, such as pillows, chair seats, or book covers, vacuum the powder off the needlework.

      This method is much less expensive than commercial dry cleaning and less damaging to surrounding hardware such as belt buckles and zippers. It really works!

Experimenting with alphabets and colors; see alphabet graphs, pages 58–84. Next page, Patches, page 95

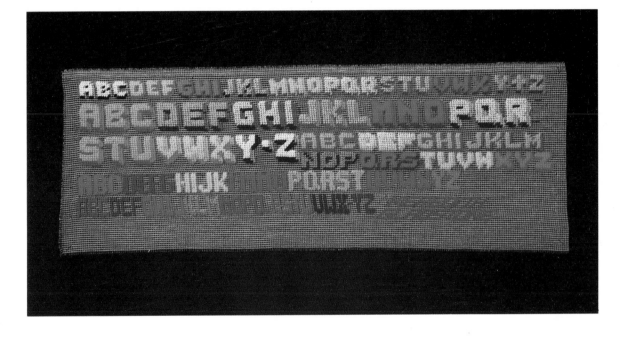

ALPHABETS

Alphabets

(Color picture 5)

A few years ago a friend, Walter Osborne, was engaged to design the look of a weekly newspaper about to be launched in a large suburb of New York. The new paper's chief competition was stolid and traditional-looking. Osborne's job was to compete with a fresh, lively, modern design that would be easy to read.

Sitting behind an enormous layout table, Osborne was weighing type styles to be used for headlines. He could be heard to mumble, "That's it! Ultra Bodoni Italic. It has a friendly, honest look." Friendly? Honest? What was he talking about? We gathered around the table as he paraded for us a number of sample headlines set in different typefaces. He asked us to select which we liked best among about five styles. None of us knew a Roman from a Gothic, let alone an Ultra Bodoni Italic. But six of us, looking for the friendly and honest one, selected Osborne's Ultra Bodoni without knowing which one it was, because compared to the others it really did look friendly and honest.

Type and ornamental alphabets are fascinatingly varied in their styles, moods, and designs. The incredible gingerbread *Lapidaire Monstre* (page 110) and the clean, classic Clarendon (page 83) are but a few of the thousands of styles of letters that can be used in needlepoint. Some letters are so handsome that their shape alone is all the design you may want to use.

To help excite your imagination, this chapter includes some samples of printed alphabets that may be used to form words, monograms, or giant initials. They can be enlarged to the size you want by free-hand graphing, by photostat, or by photoprojection (see the chapter on "Techniques"). And there are also a dozen alphabets graphed stitch for stitch so that letters can be copied directly from the printed page. Almost all the finished projects in this book—the patches and samplers and the Victorian monogram pillow in the following chapters especially—will give you an idea of what can happen when you get interested in alphabets!

57

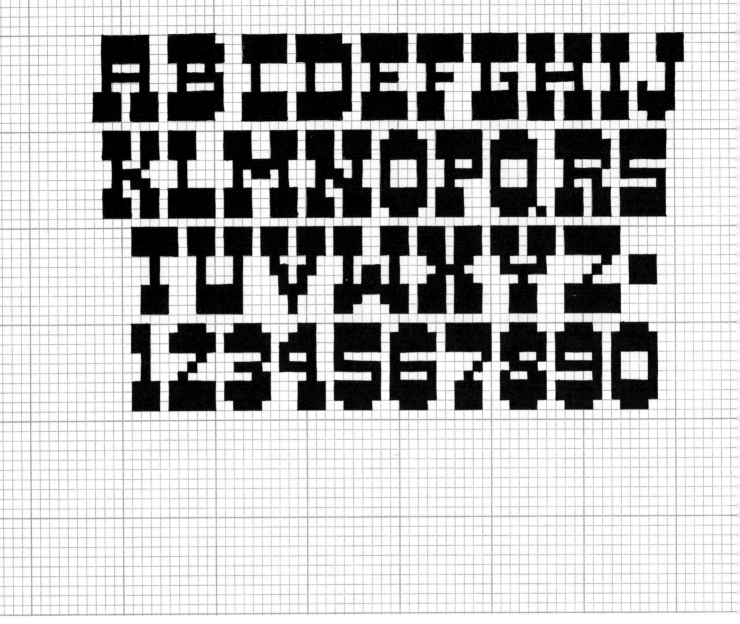

Circus

Poster

Stencil Roman

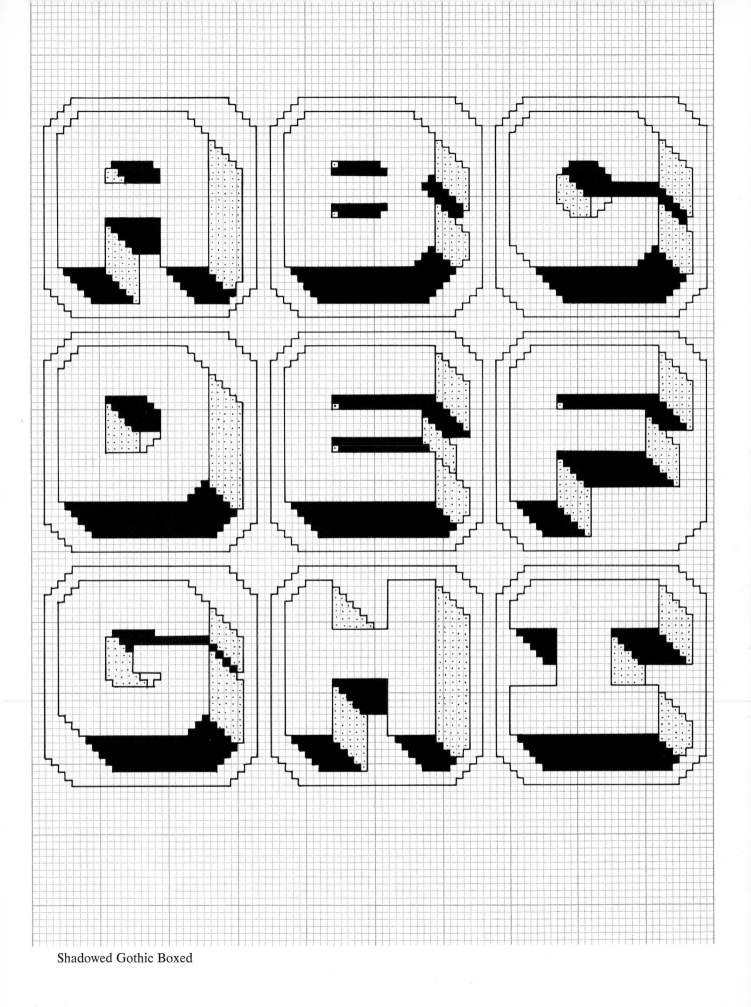

Shadowed Gothic Boxed

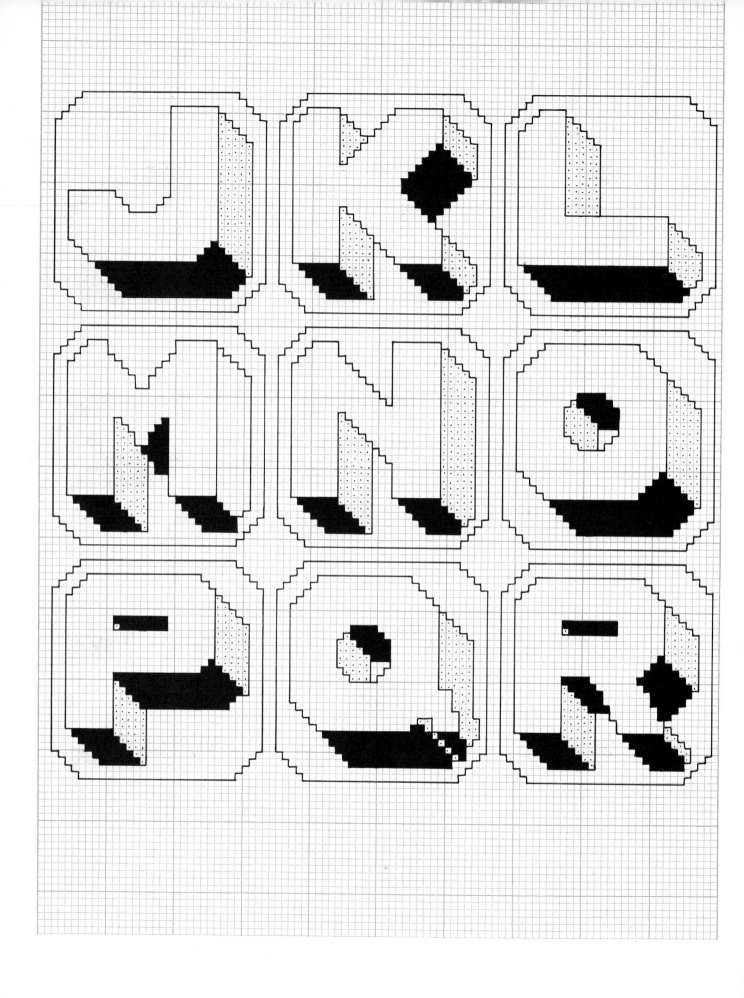

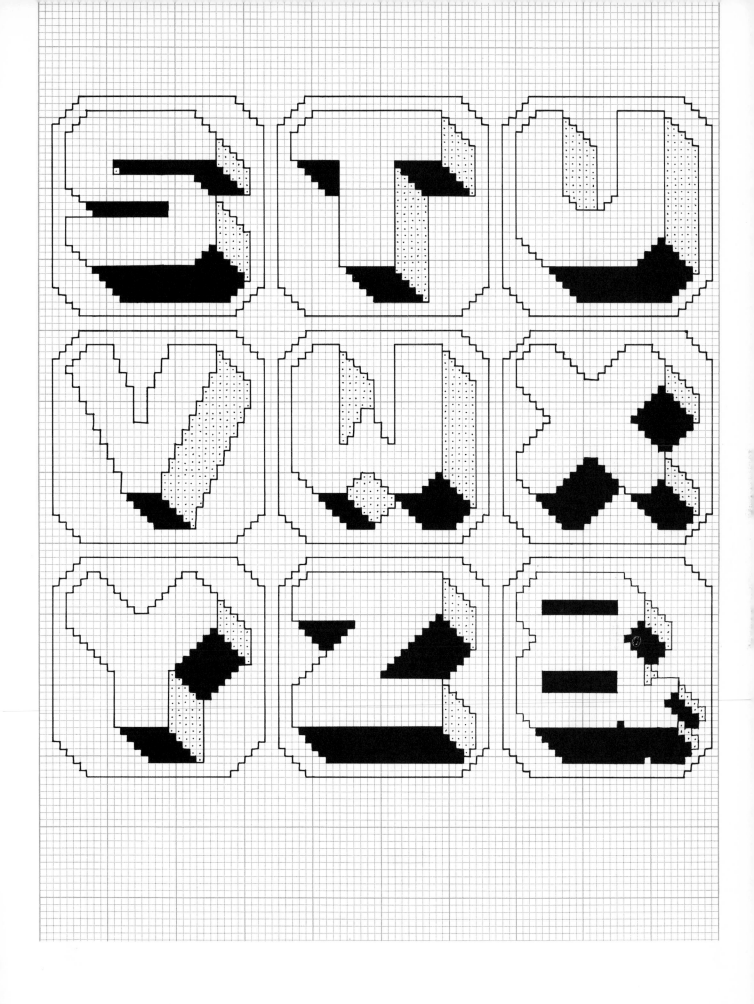

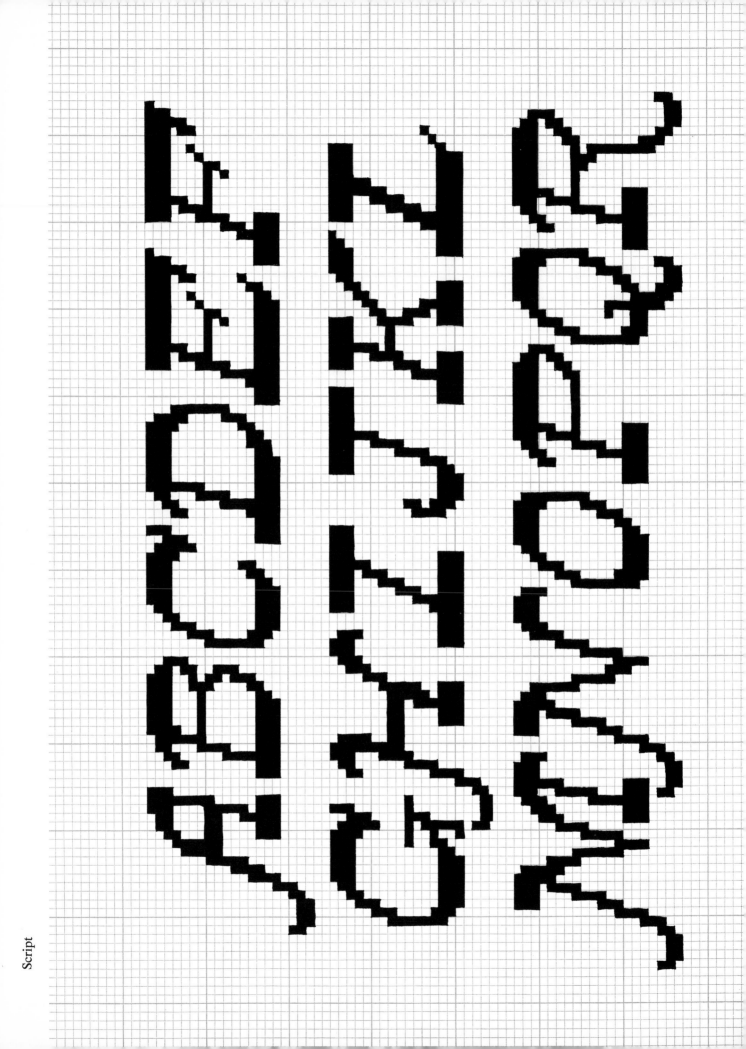

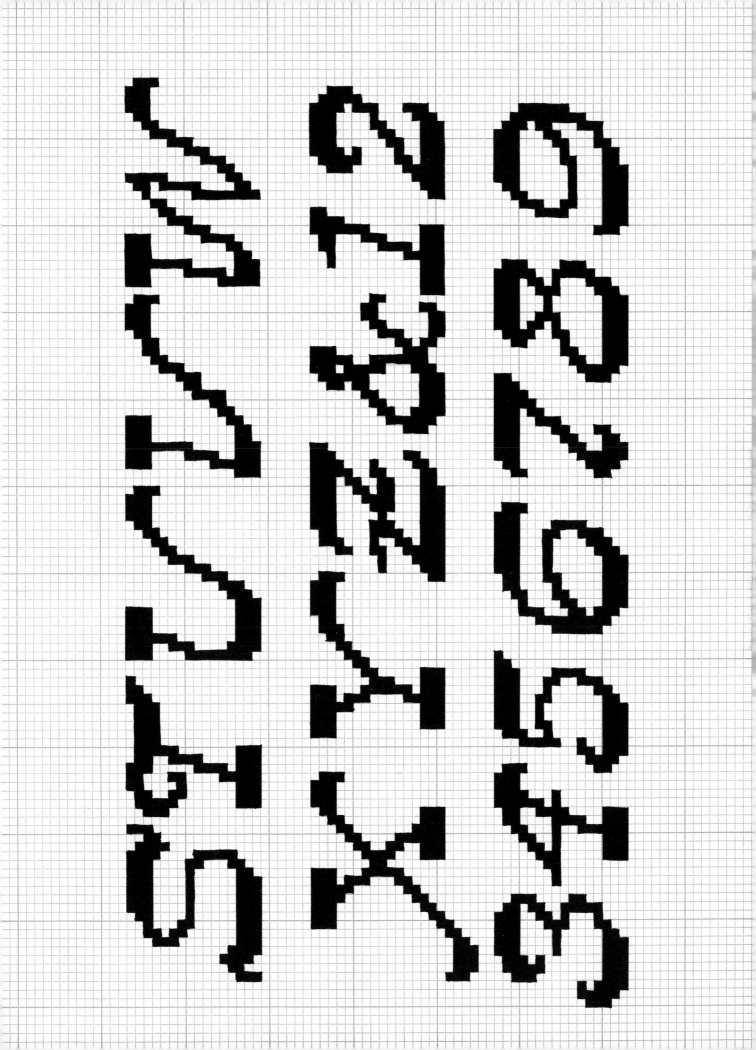

Banker's Gothic Outlined

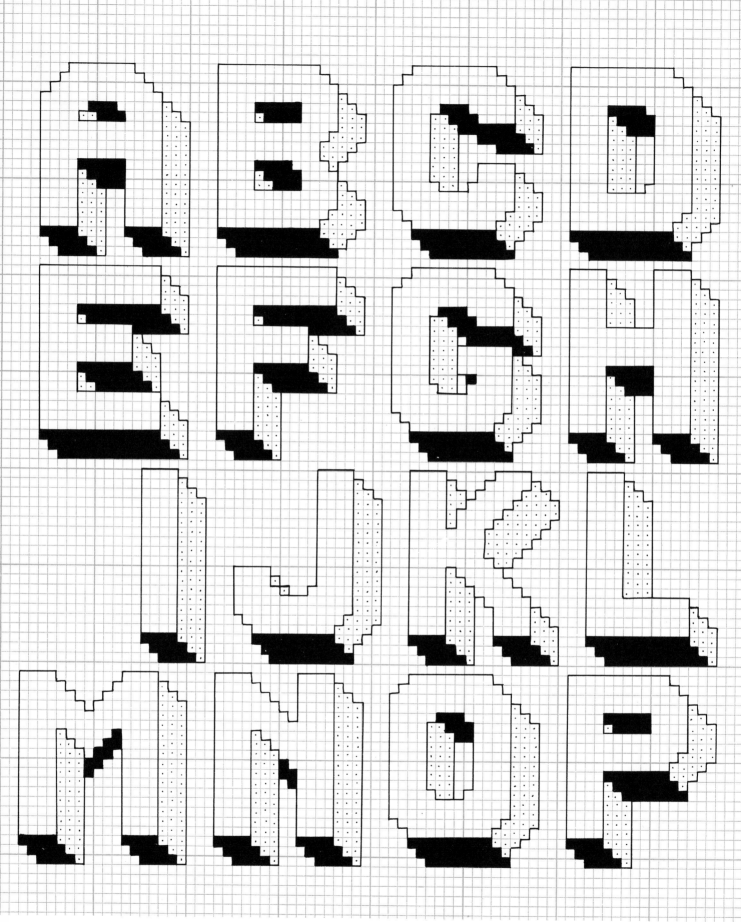

3-D

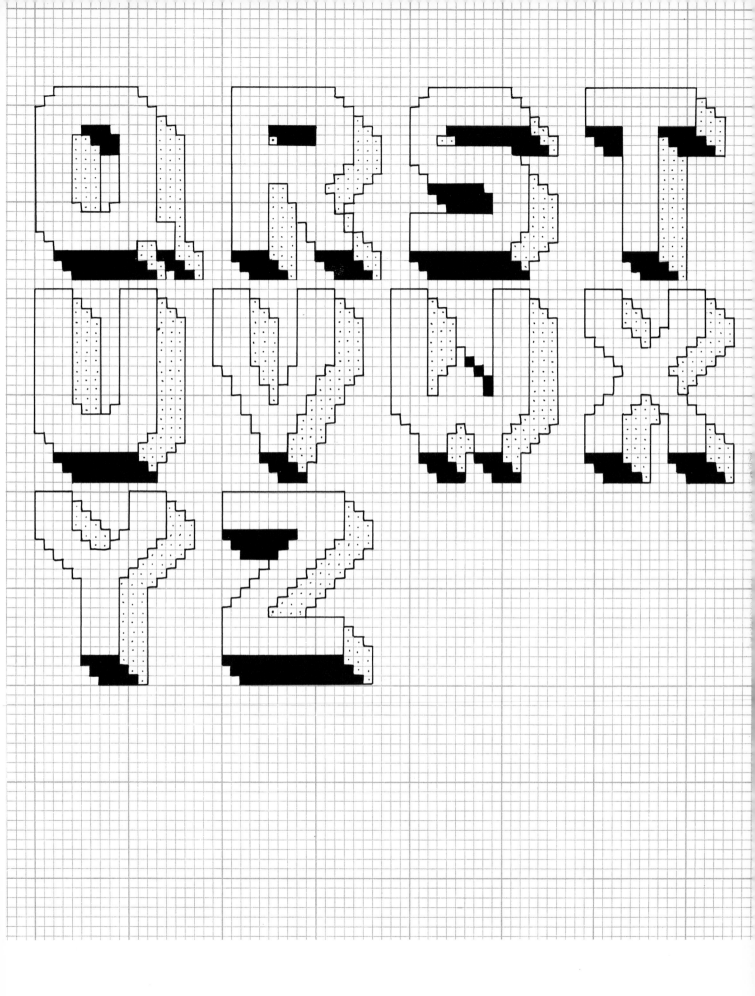

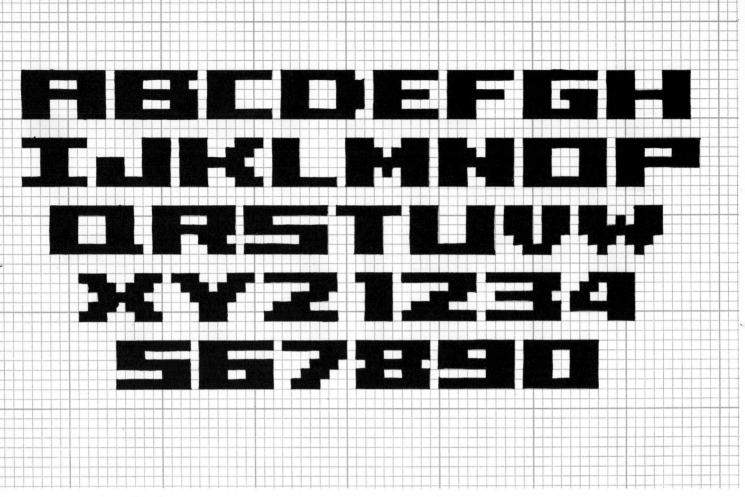

Railroad

Circus Lower-case

Lower-case Slant

Sampler: A–Z and 1–9, page 101

Shadowed Gothic

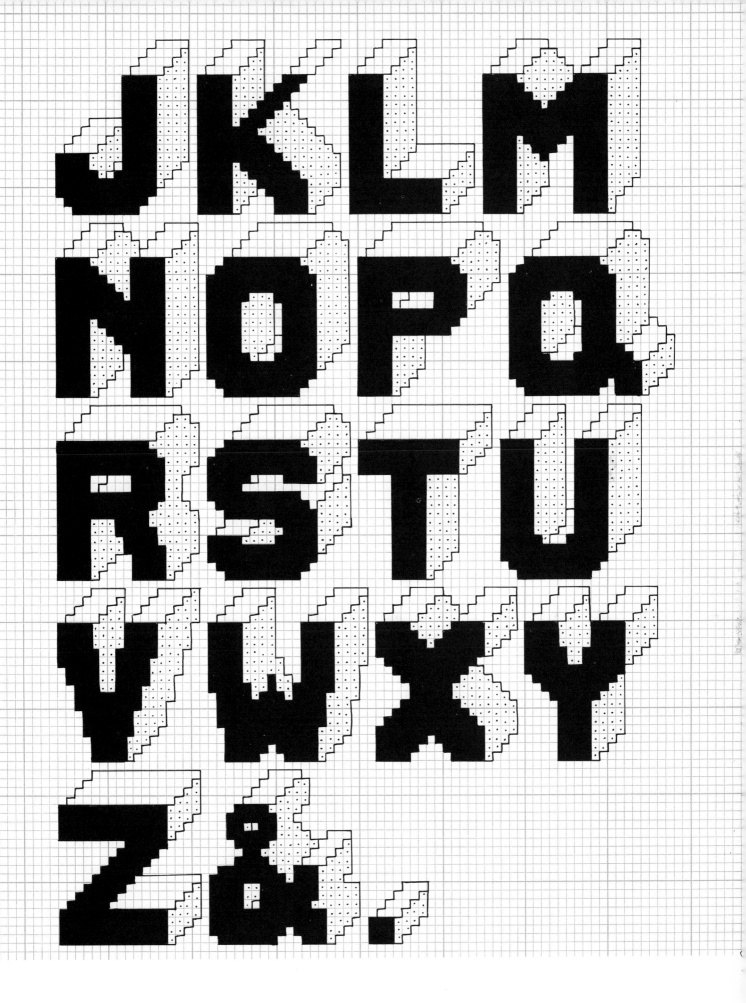

Side Show

Potpourri

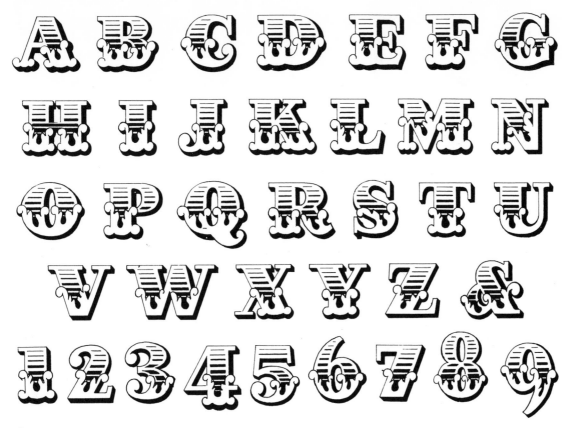

Sunset

A B C D E F G
H I J K L M N
O P Q R S T U
V W X Y Z ?

Stencil Gothic

Monograms I

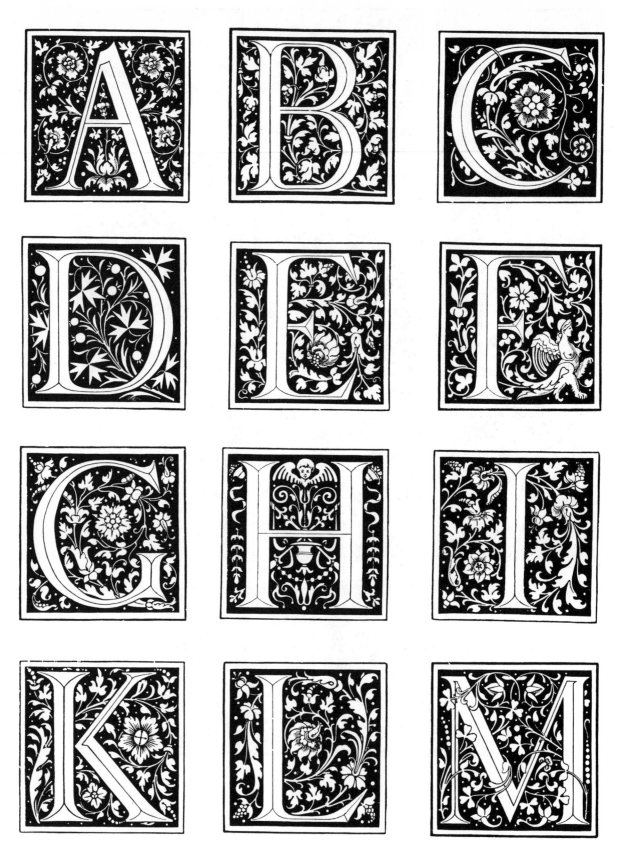

Monograms II

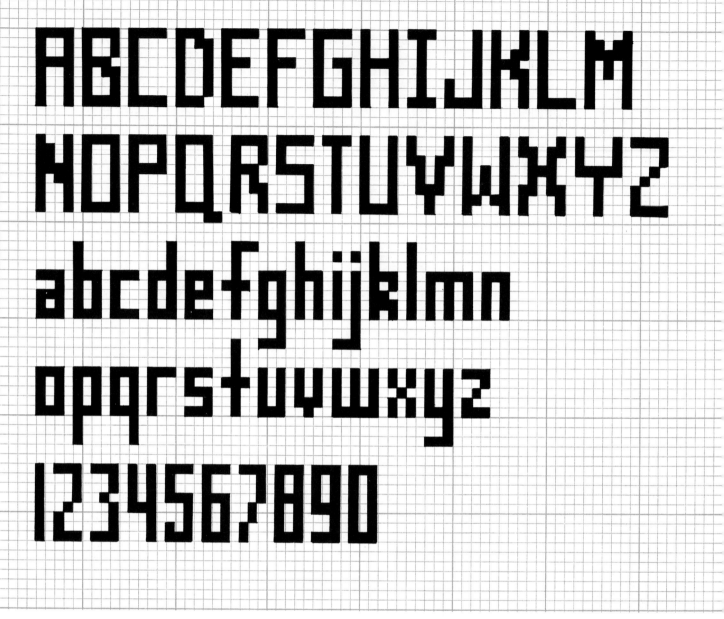

Spartan

ABCDEFG
HIJKLMN
OPQRSTU
VWXYZ &
1234567890

"Osborne" Clarendon

ABCDEF
GHIJKL?
MNOPQR
STUVWX
YZ&&123
4567890

Blueberry Gothic

ABCDEF
GHIJKL
MNOPQR
STUVW
XYZ&

"Greg" Cooper

PROJECTS

Needlepoint Tool Kit

(Color picture 4)

Who would think of serving *Vichyssoise piquante* in a Dixie cup, or presenting a gift of a diamond ring in a Baggie? How much confidence would you have if your visiting doctor pulled his stethoscope out of a brown paper bag?

Containers tell a lot about the value and importance of their contents. As a needlepoint "professional," you will have your basic tools to keep together. Instead of using a store-bought container, why not make your own elegant equipment holder? You *always* need small, sharp-pointed scissors, needles, and a thimble, and there's nothing more frustrating than having to search out each item in a separate place. Here's how to make your own personalized needlepoint tool kit. You can make it any size you wish by changing the measurements given, but otherwise the directions are the same.

MATERIALS

Penelope canvas (10/in.), 3″ wider all around than your finished measurements

Masking tape

A piece of felt the same size as the canvas

1 large fabric-covered snap

Graph paper, 10 squares per inch

Yarns, needle, thimble, scissors

The scissors you use are the largest piece of equipment to go into the holder, so make your *finished* measurement ½″ larger all around than your scissors. For instance, the scissors measure 4″ long by 2″ wide, as in

87

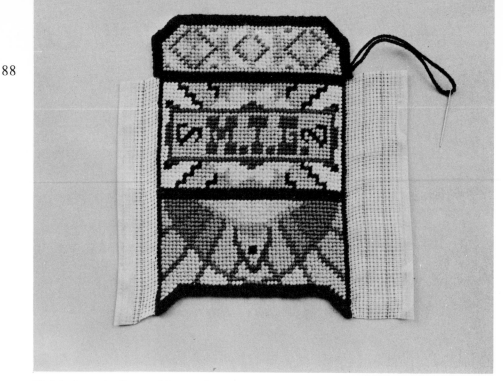

Finish clean the flap and front edges.

my diagram. Your finished measurement for the holder should be 5″ long by 3″ wide. You can lay this out directly onto canvas, but it will come out more exactly if you draw it first on graph paper.

Mark your measurements for the back side in the center of the paper. Now, *below* it, draw the front side: First, skip one space for the fold line. Then count down the same number of spaces as you did for the short ends of the back side. Count 6 spaces *in* and *up* diagonally for the diagonal corners of the top of the front, at both ends. Then draw a line straight across, connecting the diagonal corner lines.

Now draw the flap at the top, first skipping again one space for the fold line, then counting up 10 spaces. From the tenth space, count 6 spaces in and up diagonally at both ends, and draw a straight line across to connect these diagonal corners.

This is not complicated. Look at the diagram. It's adjustable to any dimensions, including a deeper front flap, but this is always the basic layout. It's all made in one piece, and when it is folded, you will have something that will look like a small purse.

Now comes the fun part—laying out your design. Take each of the three sections and plan what you would like to do in them. Make sure you lay them out so that the designs on all sides face in the right directions when you fold up the holder. The outline, stitch for stitch, of each panel is specified on the graph paper. Anything you want to design must be planned to work inside those areas, so experiment on the graph before stitching anything. Use one panel for your name or initials. Try another panel in a bargello stitch. Do a different design on every panel so that it looks like three-piece patchwork.

Victorian monogram pillow, page 105

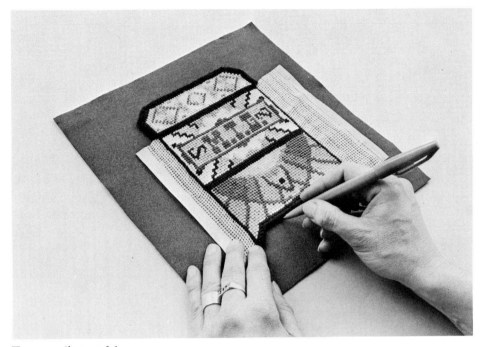

Trace outline on felt.

Use letters or numbers all over. Experiment! It's small and all the details can easily be settled on paper first. On the next page I have suggested a layout using Circus-type letters for initials on the back, though you may think the front flap is a more logical space for initials. Put anything else you think is fun in the other two areas.

Now that you have your layout, cut your canvas to the right size (a good 1½″ of spare canvas all around), bind the edges with masking tape, and stitch in your design.

When the design is finished, cut off the excess canvas around the front flap *only,* cutting between the third and fourth pairs of threads away from the needlepoint and diagonally about ⅜″ away from the corners. Fold in the canvas edges, using the first extra thread beyond the stitching as fold line, and press them between your fingers to bend them flat. Using *double* yarn, stitch around the flap, making a finished edge (see "Finishing Edges Clean," page 45). Then trim and finish the top edge on the front piece the same way. Leave the sides of the front and back taped and untrimmed until later.

Block the whole canvas so that it is squared out and the needlepoint is back to the shape of the original layout (page 43), and let it dry.

Now place it on a flat surface, right side down. Pin the felt to the back, turn over the whole thing, and mark on the felt the outlines of the finished flap, the top front edge, and the sides. Cut the felt *just* inside those outlines. Now take off the felt, and spray the wrong side of it with adhesive. Put it back on the wrong side of the finished needlepoint, and press the two together. If the felt laps over a little, you can still trim it once it is stuck.

See *Lapidaire Monstre* alphabet, page 110, for monogram pillows

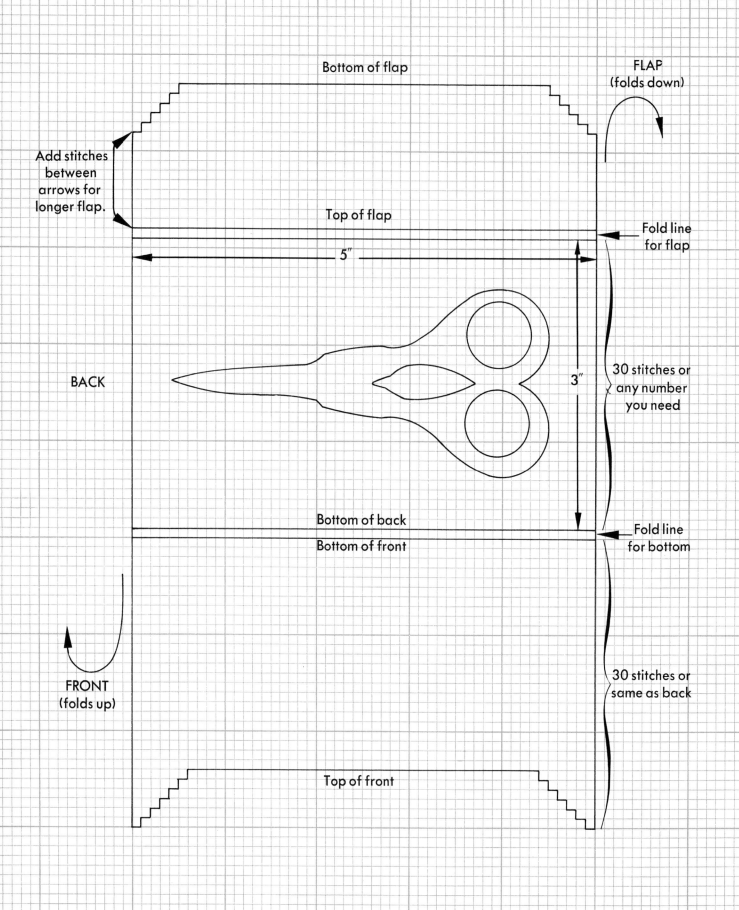

Bottom of flap

FLAP
(folds down)

Add stitches
between
arrows for
longer flap.

Top of flap

Fold line
for flap

5"

BACK

3"

30 stitches or
any number
you need

Bottom of back

Bottom of front

Fold line
for bottom

FRONT
(folds up)

30 stitches or
same as back

Top of front

Draw overall layout on graph paper.

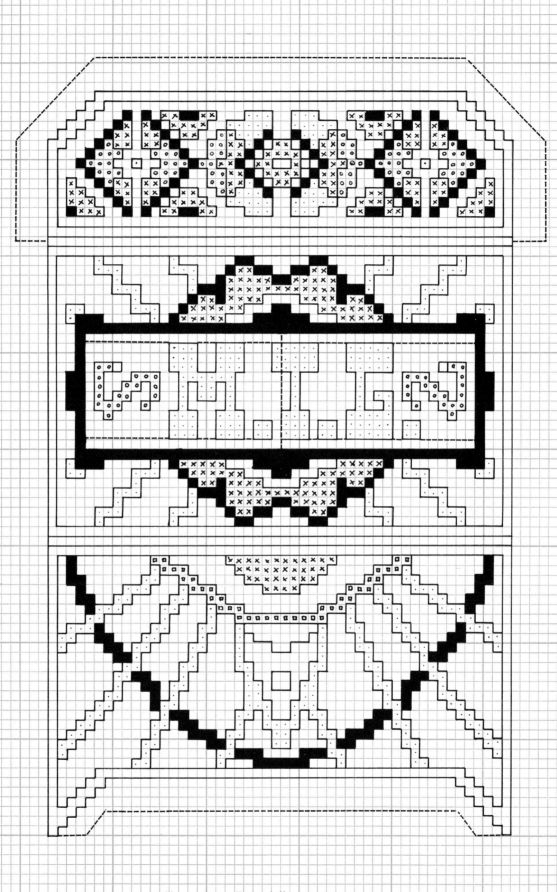

Graph design; use Circus type. Dotted line
outside flap and top of front is cutting line for
finishing.

94   Now you join the sides. Cut the canvas between the second and third lines beyond the needlepoint. Fold the front side up, following the fold line on the original diagram. With double yarn, and starting at the *bottom,* stitch the sides closed with an overcast stitch, lining up the holes of the canvas. Take an extra stitch at the top so that the seam will be reinforced, and bind off.

Fold down the flap, locate the right spot for the snap, and sew both halves of it on. Press the flap in place under a damp cloth to flatten it.

Now put your tools in! The felt backing of the flap is ideal for sticking in your needles.

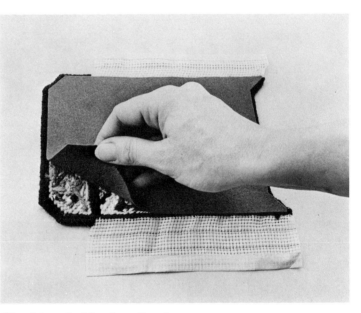

Glue felt on inside of needlepoint.

Sew snaps in place.

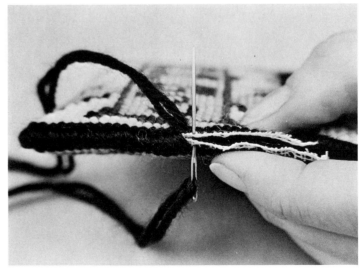

Overcast sides together.

Patches

(Color picture 6)

Blue jeans have been called the standard American youth uniform, but for years now young people have been destandardizing blue jeans and denim jackets by adding their own touches—patches, appliqués, embroidery, dyeing and bleaching, studding—anything to bring originality to these ubiquitous garments. Adults, maybe less interestingly, have been doing the same thing for years, personalizing their towels, handkerchiefs, shirts, automobiles, and mailboxes, and wearing blazers with the family crest or club emblem.

As a needlepoint artist, you are in the enviable position of being equipped to create patches to serve as monograms, emblems, or just plain ornaments on almost anything. Instead of sergeant's stripes, why not a rainbow patch for a work-jacket sleeve? Or how about a pants-pocket monogram?

MATERIALS

A piece of penelope canvas cut 1½″ larger all around than the finished size of the patch

Masking tape

Graph paper, 10 squares per inch

Yarns, needle, thimble, scissors

1. Decide on the size of the patch and then cut a piece of canvas 1½″ larger all around.
2. Bind the edges with masking tape.
3. Fold it in half and mark the center fold line with a waterproof marking pen. This marked line corresponds to the center line on the graphs.
4. On each graphed layout of the patches, there is a space for initials or a name. The alphabet to be used is identified below each graph. Decide

95

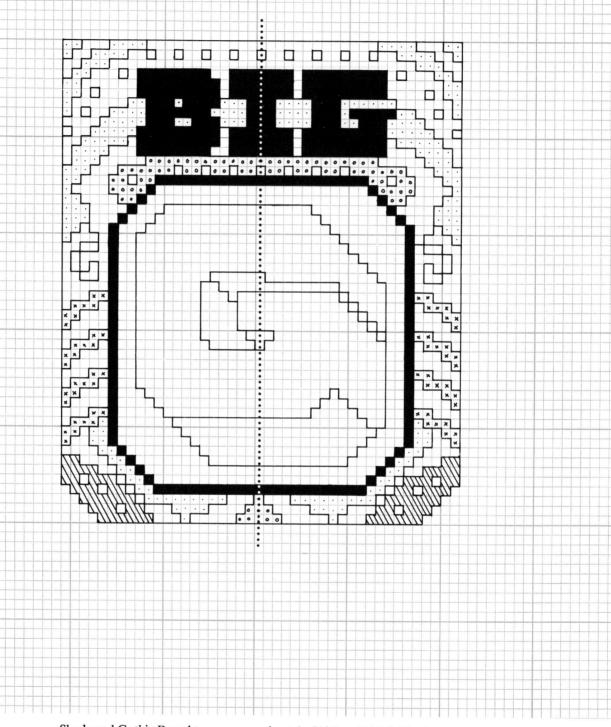

Shadowed Gothic Boxed type—approximately 5½″ × 4¾″ finished

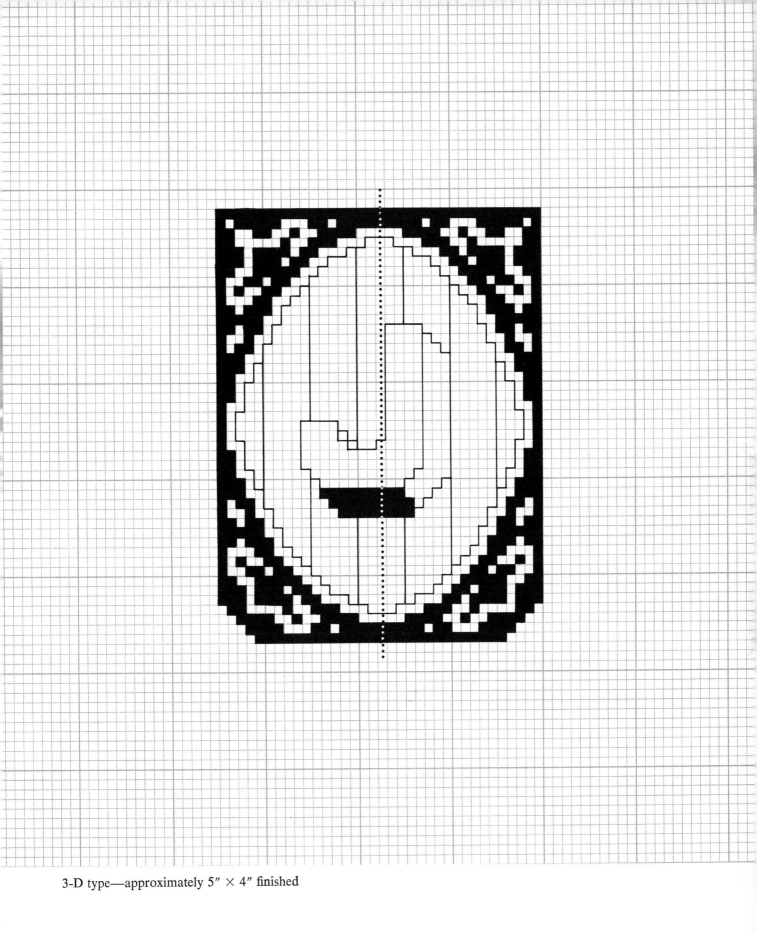

3-D type—approximately 5″ × 4″ finished

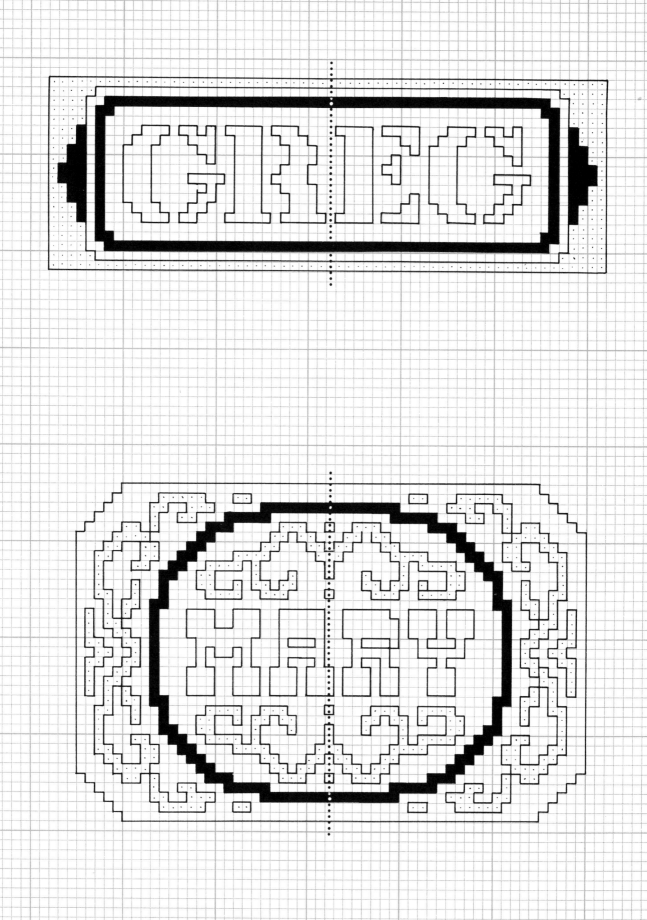

on the letters you want, and lay them out on graph paper. Suppose you want to put the name MARY on the patch: Take the letters from the Circus alphabet and draw them, space for space, on the graph paper. MARY is 31 stitches wide, so the 16th is the center line which should line up with the center line of the patch graph. (See layout of MARY patch.)

The same thing is done to lay out monograms with periods after each letter. However, do not count the last period when you are counting to find the center line. For instance, in A.B.C., count from A. to C; there are 26 stitches. In this instance, the center is between 13 and 14. Use 14, one stitch off center to the right, as the center line. The reason you do not count in the last period is that when the monogram is done, the last period would create a lopsided illusion. You are compensating by "cheating" the position of the letters. If you are not a stickler for form, eliminate the periods and simply insert small dashes on either side of the center letter, or use no periods or dashes at all.

You now have the name or initials centered in your patch. Stitch this in first, between the top and bottom guidelines, and then follow the graph for the rest of the design on the patch. Use as many colors as you want. Yarns you have left over from other projects will be perfect for this small project because you don't need much. And if you want to put a patch on something that you want to wash (such as jeans!), use Orlon or acrylic yarn.

5. To put a single letter in, use the same principle. Pick the initial you want to use from the alphabets. The guidelines for the top and bottom of the initial are already drawn, so all you need to find is the center of the letter. Count the total number of spaces it takes across for the letter and divide by two. The example is J, which is 16 spaces wide. Sixteen divided by 2 is 8. Place the 8th space on the center space marked with the dotted line, and your initial will come out even.

6. Coloring the patch: On each patch graph there is a pattern laid out showing different color areas. You can incorporate as many or as few colors as you like. The photographed patches are merely suggestions for color combinations. To finish the edges clean (page 45) all around, use double yarn of any color you want.

7. Now block the patch by squaring it out with pins in the corners and pressing it under a damp cloth, and let it dry. Then stitch the patch by hand where you want it. Use needle and thread, and with a running stitch catch the yarn on the back of the patch all around the edge to sew it to the garment.

GREG: Stencil Roman type—approximately 6½″ × 2¼″ finished. MARY: Circus type— approximately 5½″ × 3¾″ finished.

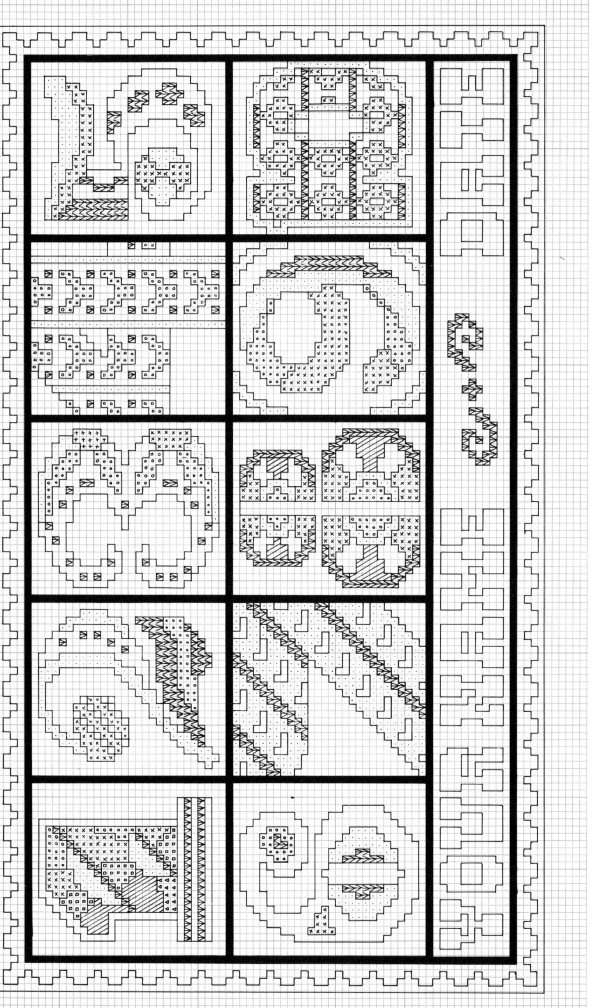

Sampler: 1–10. Use Circus type for signature and date.

Samplers: 1-10 or A-Z

(Color pictures 7 & 8)

A needlepoint sampler is traditionally made up of a variety of stitches performed on a canvas to demonstrate the craftsman's versatility. A common device has been to include an alphabet as part of the exercise. It occurred to us that, aside from a variety of stitches, samplers might deal with a variety of alphabets at once; and also that a sampling of the wide range of colors available to needlepointers coupled with assorted letter styles, borrowed or invented, could provide startling and fun-looking canvases. And while we're at it, what about numbers? Numbers have delightful shapes and contours. We're so used to thinking of numbers as mere information that we overlooked the shapes of the devices which convey the information.

The sampler in the color picture on page 17 is not graphed here partly because it would just take too many pages. We show it not as something to copy but rather to demonstrate what can be done with the mixing of all sorts of letters and colors. Each block of the sampler was graphed as the ideas came to us. It was stitched on 10/in. canvas. The blocks, inside the white dividing lines, are 40 stitches wide and 38 stitches high. And it ended up as a wall hanging—stretched on a wood panel—13″ x 40″.

We hope *somebody* will take the same idea and make a sampler rug, double the size of our panel. (The long, narrow arrangement of the blocks would not have to be the same.) This could be done in two ways: On 5/in. canvas, which would double the dimensions of each block, the stitch count would remain the same. The blocks would each be graphed as ideas for them came along. On 10/in. canvas, blocks about 8″ square would be drawn on the canvas. Then each letter would be drawn on paper rather than graphed (enlarged to fit the blocks by whatever method is most convenient) and traced onto the canvas. (To enlarge letters directly from the color picture of our sampler, see "Photographic Transfer," page 28).

It would be quite a rug. It would probably be difficult to block; get a professional to do it.

The two smaller samplers that follow may help you get started thinking about how to use the innumerable and delightful styles of lettering that can be found both in this book and in other sources.

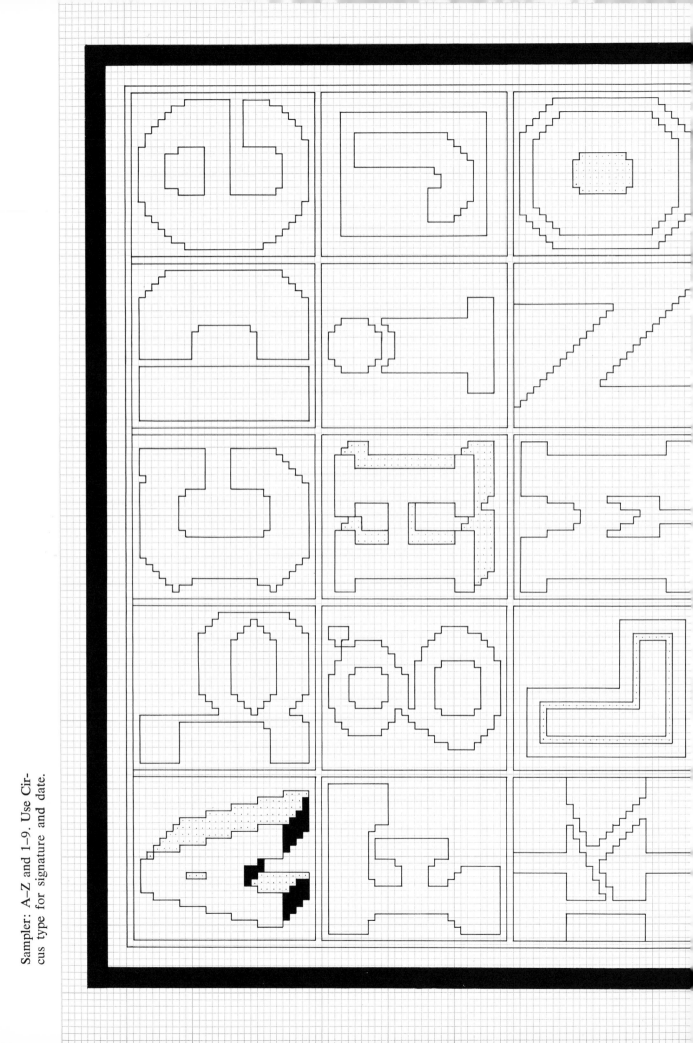

Sampler: A–Z and 1–9. Use Circus type for signature and date.

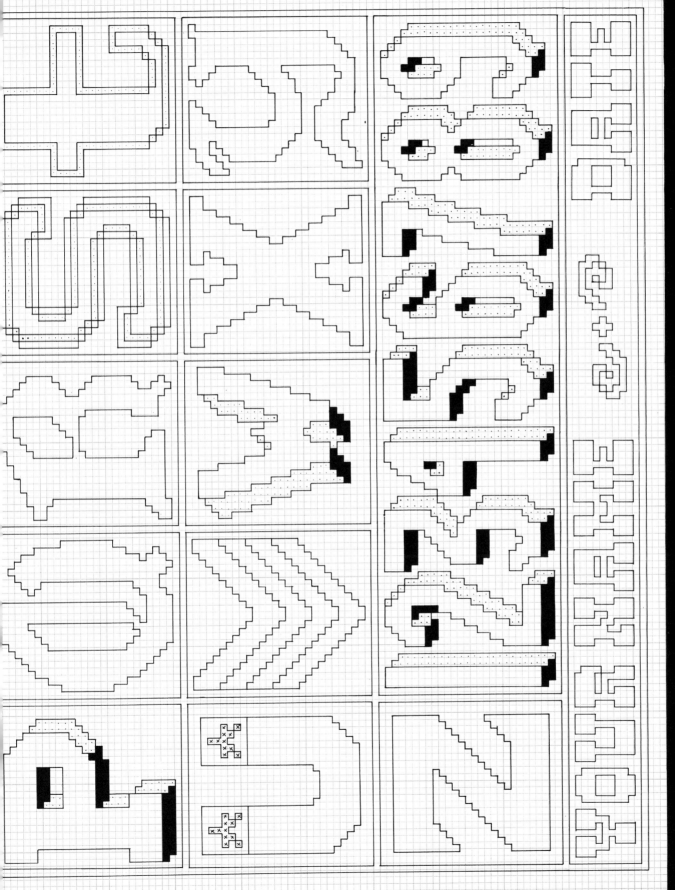

MATERIALS

Penelope or mono canvas (10/in.), cut 18″ x 24″ for the A–Z sampler, or 18″ x 12″ for the 1–10 sampler

Masking tape

Graph paper, 10 squares per inch, if you want to lay out your own letters or numbers

Yarns. Use 3-strand Persian wool, or anything that will cover your canvas

Needle, thimble, scissors

1. Cut your canvas and bind the edges with masking tape.

2. Each of the letters or numbers goes into a block 24 stitches across and 28 stitches up and down. Each block is outlined with a single row of stitches. This is the black outline on the graphed layout. Put all the outlining in first, making sure you count accurately. Then fill in each block, copying the graphed layout or drawing your own letters or numbers first on graph paper (see Step 3). For each letter or number I have given you a color breakdown on the layout, and you can refer to the color photograph (page 72). But I do suggest that you use your own color combinations, too.

3. *Making your own letters or numbers*: On the graph paper draw out blocks 24 squares across by 28 squares up and down. Sketch in the number or letter you want in pencil, then outline the design in ink, this time following the squares of the graph as closely as possible along the shape of your pencil sketch. Once the letter is inked in, you can erase all the pencil lines. Each square of the graphed outline represents one stitch of the outline of the letter or number.

You can also trace directly onto the canvas. Once you have the outlines of the blocks stitched in, place each block over a sketch of a letter or number, and trace it on the canvas. Make sure you use a *waterproof* marking pen.

4. The bottom space is your signature line. Use the lower-case Circus type (page 73). Put your name in first, going from left to right. Then put the date in, working from right to left; put the last number of the date in first, and work backward. This way your signature line will be balanced.

5. Once the entire pattern is filled in, stitch in the border. This can be as wide or as narrow as you want. It is 6 stitches wide on the layout. If you want a wider border, cut your canvas larger when you start.

6. Now block your canvas and let it dry thoroughly (page 43). I would suggest on a project like this that you have it framed.

Victorian Monogram Pillow

One of our favorite alphabets is the 19th-century *Lapidaire Monstre*. Each letter is a masterpiece of Victorian ornamentation. It's perfect for needle-pointers because so many patterns are incorporated into each letter. They can be copied quite exactly or can be interpreted to suit your own preferences.

(Color pictures 9 & 10)

The entire *Monstre* alphabet is printed here. You can have the letters enlarged to whatever size you want by taking the page to a photostatter (page 28). The larger you blow a letter up, the more detail you can put into it and the more impressive it will be. Don't let this project scare you. It's easier than it looks and once it's done everyone will think you're a genius.

MATERIALS

A photostatic enlargement of the initial you want to use: Decide what size you want the letter to be, then take this book to the photostatter. Specify the size by telling him what you want the *largest* dimension of the letter to be. Some letters are not square; always measure the longest side of the letter, whether it's the vertical or horizontal, so you won't get caught with a size that won't fit your intended space. This is a common error when one has artwork enlarged.

Canvas (10/in.), cut 4″ to 6″ larger all around than the initial (once you have the photostat, lay the canvas over it and you can judge how large to cut it)

A board and pushpins

Waterproof fine-tip marking pen

Yarns. Use 3-strand Persian wool or something comparable.

105

Graph paper, 10 squares per inch

Masking tape

Needle, thimble, scissors

1. Lay canvas over the photostat of the letter and approximate the size to cut your canvas by allowing background space plus extra canvas all around. Cut the canvas and bind the edges with masking tape.

2. You will need a hard surface, such as a drawing board, large enough to put your photostat and canvas on so you can trace the letter. Place the photostat on the board, then place your canvas on top of it, making sure the letter is centered on the canvas. Also make sure the horizontal and vertical lines of the letter line up with the horizontal and vertical threads of the canvas. Once canvas and photostat are lined up, secure them both to the board with pushpins in each corner.

With a fine-point waterproof marking pen, trace the letter: Trace the outline first, then the shadow, and last the detail inside. Here is where you can improvise. You are after an effect, so don't worry if your pattern isn't exact. You can sketch it roughly and still change it once you start filling it in with yarn. Where there is a space for small lettering inside the letter, just trace the outline of the space. This will be the nameplate. You can lay out your own letters on graph paper once the outline of the space is stitched in and counted. You now have a rough layout for the letter. Remove the pushpins and save your stat for reference.

Trace photostated letter onto canvas.

Luggage tags, page 113

Outline the letter with two rows of stitching.

3. Start stitching in your letter. The first thing to do, using white yarn, is to outline the letter all around with 2 rows of stitches. Keep all horizontal and vertical lines straight even if they don't follow your tracing line exactly.

4. Now fill in all the area of black shadow outside the letter. You now have the entire shell of the letter.

5. The next thing to do is the nameplate. Outline the nameplate space with one row of stitches all around, using any color yarn you wish. Once this border is in, count the number of threads inside the area and lay it out on graph paper. Figure out the name, initials, or whatever else you want on the graph paper, and then transfer it to the canvas in yarn. Put the letters in first, then fill in the background of the nameplate.

6. Now comes the fun. Fill in the rest of the letter with patterns. Use as many colors as you can. This is a great project for using up scraps of leftover yarn, because the more colors and patterns you have, the livelier the letter when it's completed. If you find you cannot fill in the pattern exactly as you have traced it, improvise. You can't make a mistake, so enjoy taking chances.

7. When the letter is complete, you can pick a color to fill in the background. Make the background any size you wish; just make sure there is enough of it so that your finished letter really shows up and practically jumps off the canvas. Once a background is done, do four to ten rows of a border color to frame the letter and add a finishing touch.

8. Now block the canvas (page 49) and leave it to dry completely.

9. You can now back the needlepoint and make a pillow (page 49), or you can frame it. Whatever you do with it, this is one project that is completely your own and which you can be very proud of.

Sign, page 123

Lapidaire Monstre

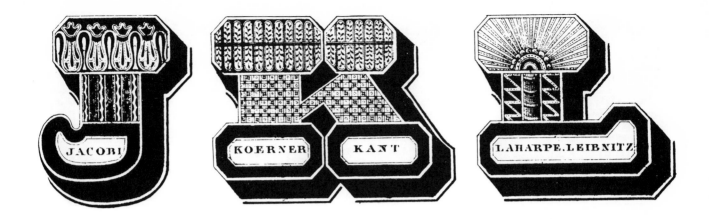

JACOBI KOERNER KANT LAHARPE.LEIBNITZ

Mozart MEIERBEER Nicolai Newton OBERLIN

PERRAULT QUINAULT RABELAIS Rossini

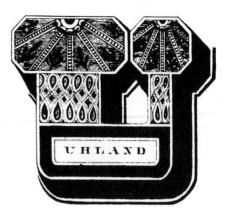

Lapidaire Monstre

Luggage Tag

(Color picture 11)

Recently on a business trip, I stood waiting at the airport luggage ramp, where the bags from the flight were circling in front of the waiting passengers on the carousel, a device common to many airports. As I saw my bag coming around the bend, resplendent with a needlepoint luggage tag Meredith had made for me with my initials on it and a bright rainbow-colored flame stitch, I heard two couples remark, "Look at that!" Feeling great pride, I decided to let the bag make one more trip around the carousel to distinguish itself with its beautiful tag before I reached over to pluck it from the conveyor. Had I been even more of an awful show-off, I might have let the bag circle for the rest of the afternoon.

Here is how you can make your own personalized luggage tag.

MATERIALS

Penelope canvas (10/in.), 10″ long by 3½″ wide (cut longer if you want more than 3 initials; allow 1¼″ more for each additional letter)

Masking tape

Waterproof marking pen

Watchband or buckle strap about ½″ wide

Yarns, needle, thimble, scissors

1. Cut out your canvas and bind the edges with masking tape.
2. Fold canvas in half and, with a waterproof marking pen, draw a vertical line on the center fold. (This is the fold line between the two sides of the tag.) Fold canvas in half horizontally, and draw a line on this fold. (This is the guideline for the middle of the letters.)

113

3. *Not* counting the vertical center thread, count 5 lines to the right and mark that thread. This is the line on which you start the letters. The letters are 9 threads high, so mark the threads 4 lines above and 4 lines below the horizontal center thread. These are the guidelines for the top and bottom of the letters. Use the Circus-type alphabet (page 58). Look at the graphed letters and stitch them onto the canvas, using the guidelines for placement. Now fill in the background, going one row of stitches outside the letters all around. Take another color of yarn and stitch a row all around the background block to make the first stripe of the border.

Mark vertical and horizontal fold lines.

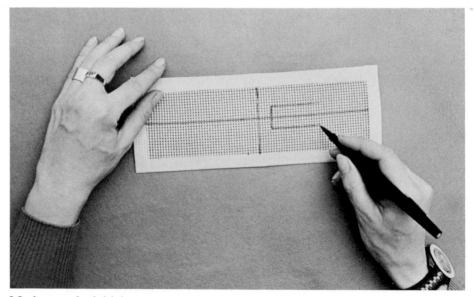

Mark space for initials.

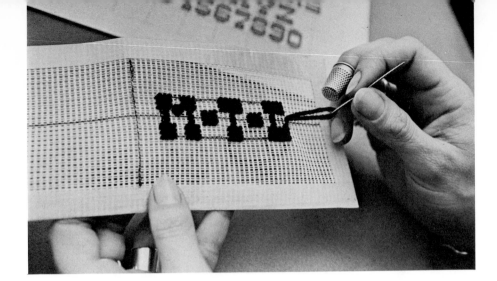

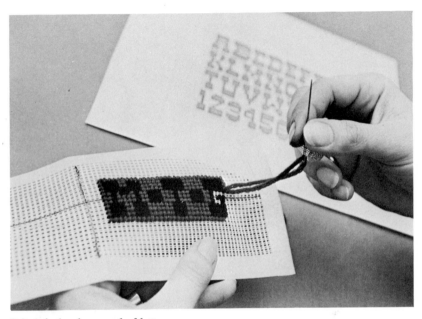

Stitch in background of letters.

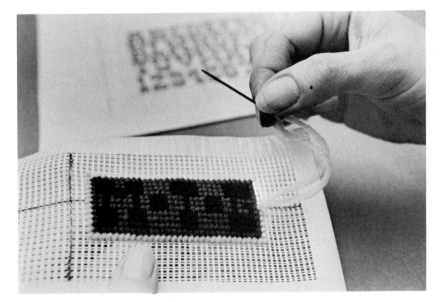

Stitch border around letter box.

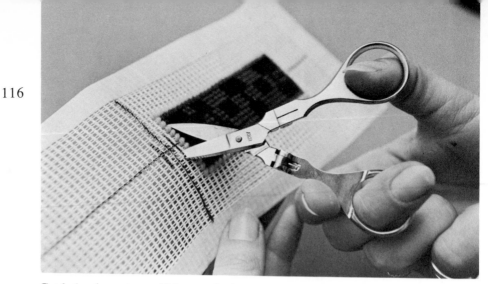

Cut hole where strap will be attached.

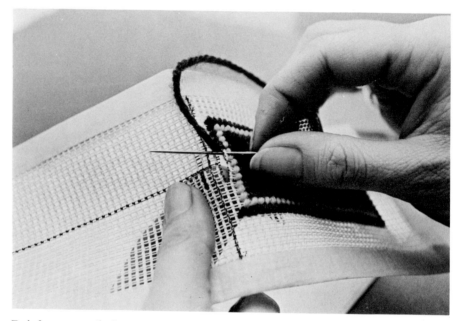

Reinforce strap hole.

4. Between the first and second threads to the right of the vertical center thread, cut vertically through the middle 5 horizontal threads. Do this on both the right and left sides of the center thread. You should have 3 center threads between the cuts.

5. Put another row of stitches around the block of letters. This is the second stripe; where you have cut the canvas in the center, continue the stripe along the single canvas thread so that the cut will have a finished edge. The right side is now finished. Count the total number of stitches across the top row of the complete block, and note the amount.

Opposite: Birthday box, page 127

Next page: Belts, page 133

6. Count 2 threads to the left of the original vertical center thread, and mark. Using this as the first thread, count to the left the amount of stitches noted for the top of the right-hand block, and mark. Extend the top and bottom lines of the block from right to left, making guidelines for an identical left-hand block. Stitch a row all around on these guidelines, continuing the stitch where the canvas has been cut in the center. The left side is now completely outlined. Fill in this space with the bargello stitch or anything else you would like.

7. Now the excess canvas must be cut off so that the tag can be finished. Cut all around between the second and third threads after the last row of stitches.

8. Fold the tag in half along the original vertical fold line. Using *double* yarn, join both sides together with an overcast stitch, matching up the holes of canvas, and covering both lines of canvas threads all around. Where the threads have been cut at the center, continue the stitch over the separated center threads to make a buttonhole loop for the strap to go through.

9. Pin the tag on a board, squaring it out with a pin in each corner. Press it under a wet cloth, and allow it to dry.

10. Now put the strap through the buttonhole opening, and the tag is ready for a suitcase, briefcase, pocketbook, or anything else you might like to attach it to.

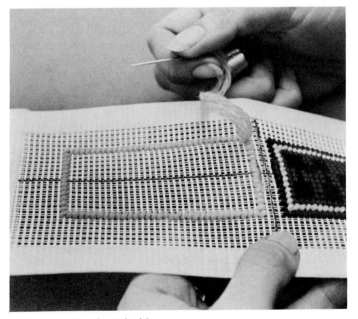

Stitch in outline for left side.

Fill in left side with a bargello pattern.

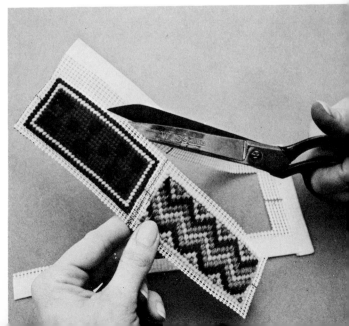

Hats, page 141

Join sides together with overcast stitch, matching canvas holes.

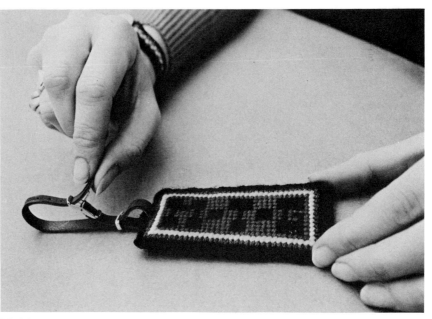

Finished luggage tag

Sign

In our apartment-office, the coat closet is next to the front door. Ever since (Color picture 12) we have occupied this apartment, callers have been waving their goodbyes and smilingly stepping into our closet. It happened so many times that we thought of painting a giant arrow to help people avoid this embarrassing exit. However, we found instead an antique wooden hand with a pointing finger that must have been part of an old store sign. We hung it on the closet door with the finger pointing to the front door next to it. People still walk into the closet, but at least they have been forewarned.

The hand, an intriguing example of American sign art, was obviously copied from a printer's slug or woodcut used in poster printing. We've designed a needlepoint version that says THIS WAY OUT, but a number of other appropriate messages could be put on it. Framed and hung in the right spot, it can serve some useful purpose other than merely showing off your needlepoint artistry. It might say: GO AWAY, EXIT, OVER THERE, TO THE JOHN, KITCHEN, TEDDY'S ROOM, DUNGEON, WIPE YOUR FEET, or TO THE POOL.

MATERIALS

Canvas (10/in.), a piece 21″ wide by 16″ high

Graph paper, 10 squares per inch, if you wish to design your own message

Masking tape

Yarns, needle, thimble, scissors

NOTE: The placement of colors is given on the layout. Refer also to the color photo, or use your own color scheme.

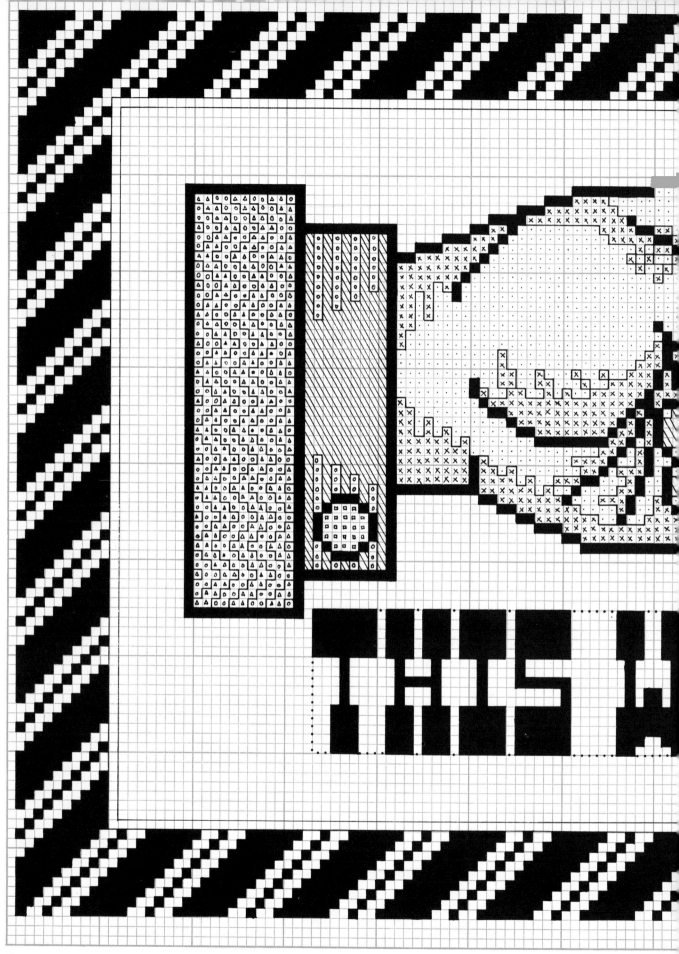

Graphed layout of sign. Use Poster type.

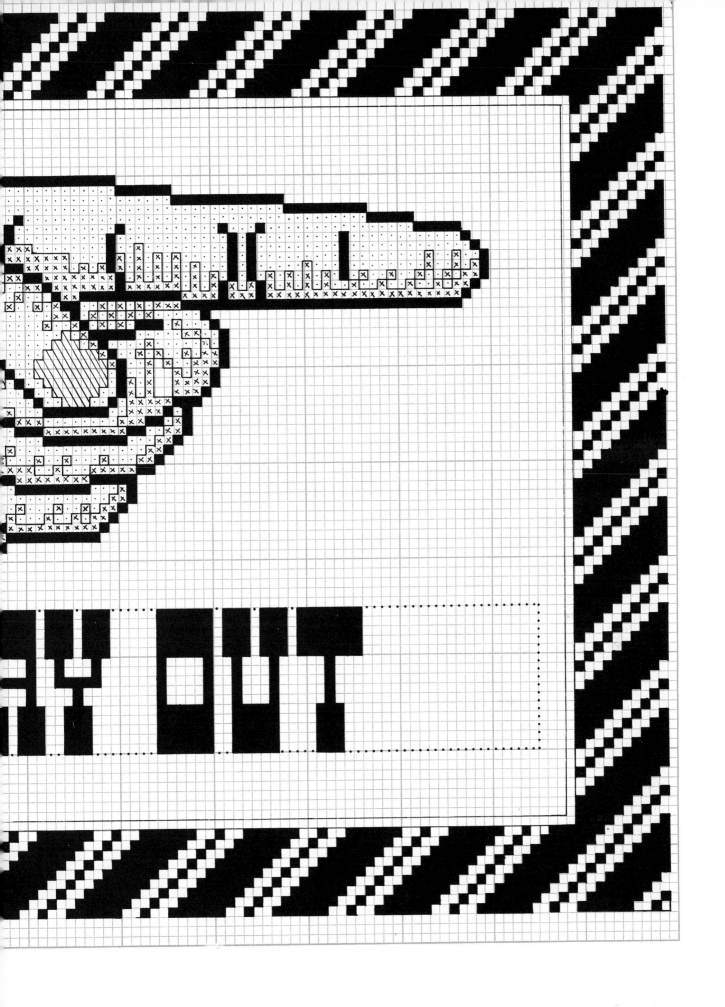

1. Cut your canvas and bind the edges with masking tape. Twenty-one inches by 16″ allows about 3″ extra canvas on each side. If you want a larger sign, allow more canvas and continue the pattern for the border as far out as you want.

2. Refer to the layout and stitch in the outline of the hand first. Your guidelines for placement would be about 4¾″ down from the top of the canvas and about 4¾″ in on each side. Fill in the details of the hand.

3. Below the hand there are guidelines for the line of type. You can put in any message you want. Just make sure that the lettering fits inside the decorative border. Check by laying it out on graph paper and counting the spaces it will take. Use the Poster alphabet (page 59). For instance, THIS WAY OUT takes 83 spaces. There is a total of 102 spaces allowed, so anything that goes beyond that will not fit.

4. Now stitch in the border and then the background.

5. Block the canvas, frame it, and hang it in an appropriate spot. This could also be a pillow, saying something such as DO NOT SIT! Whatever you make, have fun.

Birthday Box or Date Box

MATERIALS

(Color picture 13)

A clear plastic cube (such as a Graphicube, by Graphicana, Ossining, New York), open on one side and measuring approximately 3¾″ each way. The cube is made with a foam-rubber-block or cardboard-box insert to hold snapshots.

Penelope canvas (10/in.)

Graph paper, 10 squares per inch

Masking tape

Yarns, needle, thimble, scissors

1. Cut a piece of canvas 16″ x 16″, and bind the edges with masking tape.
2. Fold the canvas in half both vertically and horizontally, and mark the fold lines on the canvas threads. The point where the fold lines cross is the center of your canvas and corresponds to the crossing dotted center lines on the graph. This is the center of the top of the cube.
3. *Not* counting the marked center thread lines, count 16 thread lines up, down, to the left, and to the right. Mark along the 16th threads on all four sides. This is the top of the cube—a total of 33 threads square.
4. Now extend each of these lines out for about 4″. On the extended lines count out 33 threads on each, and mark the 33rd line. Now you have the entire flat layout for the cube on canvas. It will look like this:
5. In the center square, stitch in the graphed design for "Date Box" on page 131. Each of the other four squares is to have a single-line border all around; put the borders in now.

127

6. Now you have four squares left to fill in with whatever you want. My design is for a short name and a date repeated on all four sides of the cube. If both a name and date won't fit, use initials. Or put a single initial on three of the sides and the date on the fourth (see "Patches" on page 95 for how to center a single letter in a space). Use your imagination, don't be afraid to improvise, and play with designs on graph paper first. I shall explain how to fit a short name and a date in a square:

7. Each square is 31 x 31 stitches (two threads have been used for the borders). Draw a square on graph paper 31 x 31 spaces on each side. (Draw four squares if each side of the cube is to have a different design.) Mark the crossing center lines (the 16th lines):

Now lay out the name and date: Divide the square into three rows as shown on the layout. Each row is nine spaces wide so they will fit this way:

$$\begin{array}{rl} 1 & \text{space} \\ 9 & \text{spaces} \\ 1 & \text{space} \\ 9 & \text{spaces} \\ 1 & \text{space} \\ 9 & \text{spaces} \\ \underline{1} & \text{space} \\ 31 & \text{spaces in all} \end{array}$$

Use the Circus alphabet (page 73). Center the name or initials on the first line. From the alphabet graph, count out the number of spaces for each letter, plus one space in between each letter. I shall use GREG as an example:

$$\begin{array}{cccc} G & R & E & G \\ 5 + 1 + 6 + 1 + 5 + 1 + 5 \end{array}$$

which equals 24. Twenty-four divided by 2 is 12, and the right-hand side of R will be the twelfth space. Put the R on the graph and then fill in the rest of the letters with one space between each. Use this method for laying out each line of the design before you transfer it to canvas (it's easier to fix things on paper than on canvas).

If each square is to be different, lay them all out on paper using this technique. Always lay out the line of type first, find the center, place it within the top and bottom guidelines, and match the center line of the type to the center line of the square.

8. Stitch all the squares (the first illustration shows the directions in which the stitches in each square should go), then block the canvas back into shape (page 43).

9. Now trim off the extra canvas, leaving about ¾″ all around the finished work. The dotted outline in the illustration is the cutting line.

Box box. Directions for covered boxes, page 149

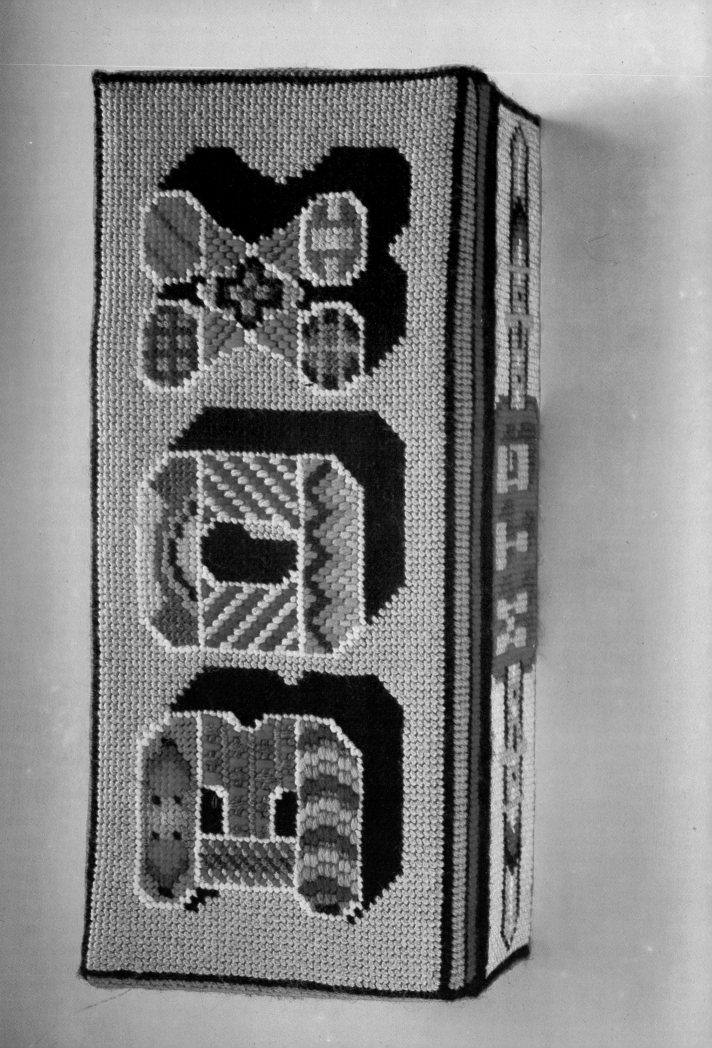

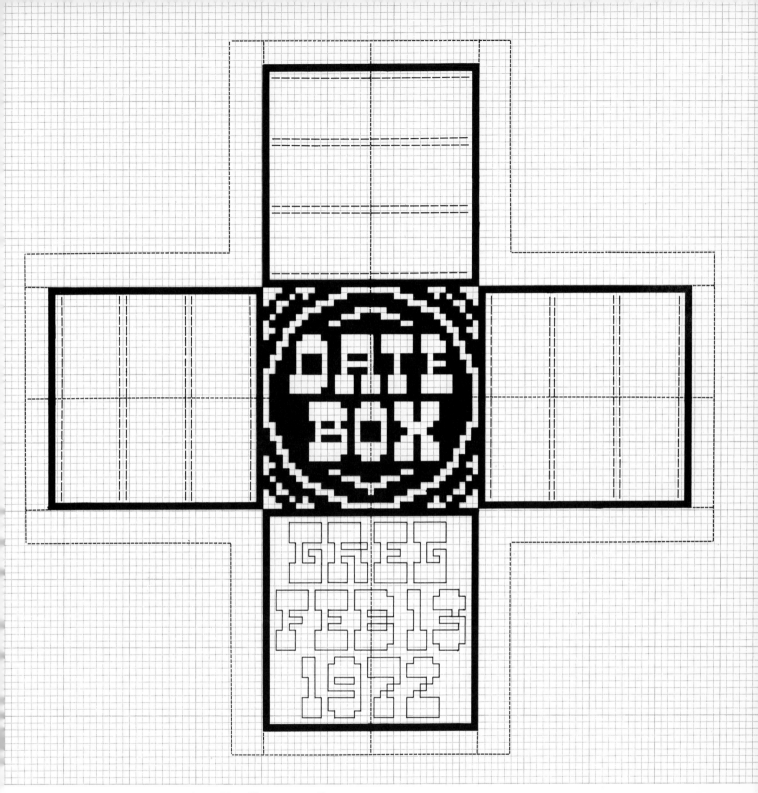

Graphed layout of date box. Use Circus type. Cut
along dotted outlines when needlepoint is done.

Covered box, page 149

10. At each corner, put the right sides of the canvas together, and sew them together with yarn and needle, using a straight basting stitch. Close the seams starting at the *top* of each, making sure you line up the holes of the canvas evenly so that the two sides of the seam will match at the bottom. Stitch only as far down as the last stitch of the needlepoint.

11. Snip corners of seams and press open with your fingers, then tack raw canvas back with needle and thread so seams will stay flat. Now turn the finished work right side out.

12. The bottom edges of the cube now must be finished clean (see page 45).

13. Then stuff the needlepoint inside the plastic cube. Cut five pieces of cardboard 3¼″ x 3¼″, and push them inside the needlepoint—one on each side and one lining the top. Now put in the piece of foam rubber to hold everything in place.

Sew seams, right sides of needlepoint together.

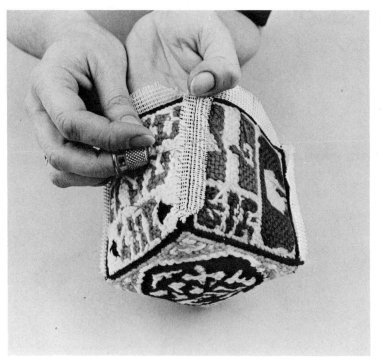

Tack raw canvas back with needle and thread so seams will be flat.

Belts

MATERIALS

(Color pictures 14 & 15)

Penelope canvas (10/in.)

For the buckle belt, a piece of canvas, cut along the selvage, 5″ wide by your waist measurement plus 10″. *Example*: If your waistline measures 26″, add 10″ to the canvas, making it a total of 36″ in length. Cut the canvas 5″ wide by 36″ long.

For adjustable or tie belt, a piece of canvas 5″ wide by your waistline measurement plus 1″. *Example*: If your waistline measures 26″, add 1″ to the canvas, making it a total of 27″ in length. Cut the canvas 5″ wide by 27″ long.

NOTE: If you want to make a wider or narrower belt, cut your canvas 3″ to 4″ wider overall than whatever you want the finished width to be.

A buckle and eyelets for the buckle belt. Buckles usually come in standard sizes, so it's a good idea to decide ahead which size buckle you will use, in order to make your belt the proper width. The belt I have described requires a 1¾″ buckle. In a notions department or sewing-supplies store, you can find eyelet kits. There are several makers, but the one most satisfactory is the large eyelet kit made by Scovill.

Or, about 2 yards of ribbon or leather ties for the adjustable tie belt. If you want yarn ties, make sure you have enough extra yarn to crochet or braid two lengths each 21″ long, plus enough for tassels. Anything else you may like is fine. Try shopping in the ribbon department for some interesting braid or embroidered ribbon. Ribbons or braid may even inspire a design for the belt.

Backing for the belt—a piece of felt, ribbon, or leather as long and wide as your finished belt

133

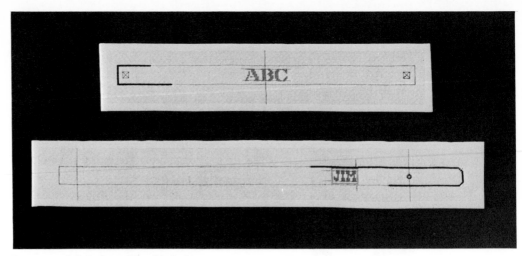

Layouts of tie belt and buckle belt

Yarns, needle, thimble, scissors

Masking tape

Graph paper, 10 squares per inch

Once you have determined which style of belt you want to make, cut your canvas according to the directions given above in the list of materials, and bind all the edges with masking tape. Remember, you must use penelope canvas.

LAYOUT FOR BUCKLE BELT

Now you can mark your guidelines on the canvas. If you want to use the Stencil Roman type (page 60), your belt should be 16 threads wide, so measure up about 1¾" from the long bottom edge of the canvas, and mark that thread line all the way across. Then count up to the 16th thread line above, and mark that line all the way across. For the Circus type (page 58) or Railroad type (page 70), your belt should be 15 threads wide. Whatever type you use, the belt should be 6 stitches wider than the height of the type (3 stitches extra above and below).

At the right-hand end of the canvas, measure in about 1¾" to the left, and mark that thread line. This will be the finished end of your belt. Measure in 4¼" to the left from the finished-end mark, and mark again. This will be where you put your *center* eyelet. Starting from this point, measure the correct waist measurement all the way to the left, and mark that with a vertical line. This line is the fold line where you will bend back the canvas to put the buckle on. Measure another 1½" to the left of the buckle line, and mark. This 1½" is the tab to be bent back to secure the buckle.

Now pick one color and do one row of stitches around the edges of the whole belt. All the guidelines along the belt are marked, so now you can fill in with needlepoint. The bargello stitch is a great one to use, covering 2 threads with one stitch, and there are several patterns illustrated. Try one of these, or make up your own.

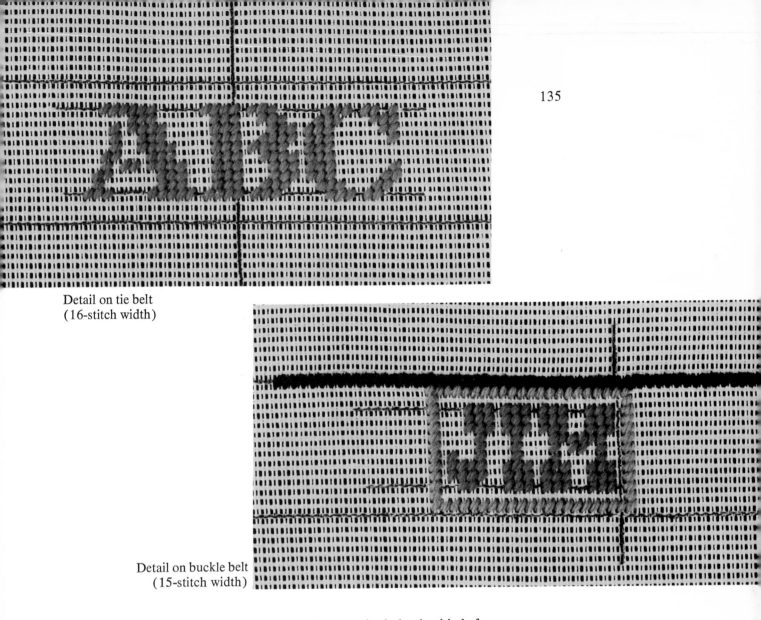

Detail on tie belt
(16-stitch width)

Detail on buckle belt
(15-stitch width)

If you want to put a name or initials on the belt, do this before you fill in the overall pattern. From the right-hand finished end of your belt, measure to the left 8½″ and mark the vertical thread line. This is the guideline for the right-hand side of the *last* letter or initial. Count the spaces from the top to bottom guidelines on the graph for the alphabet you have chosen, and draw the same guidelines on the canvas, centered between the top and bottom of the belt. Start with the last letter and work in the name or initials backward, reading each letter from your graphed alphabet. Now stitch in a border all around the name or initials. Then you can fill in the rest of the belt with whatever pattern you want.

LAYOUT FOR ADJUSTABLE TIE BELT

When your canvas is ready (page 27), fold the belt in half and mark the vertical fold line. This marks the center back of the belt. Your finished belt should be 2″ shorter than your waistline measurement. *Example*: If the waist measurement is 26″, your belt should finish at 24″. To mark your guidelines for the ends of the belt, measure 12″ to the left of the center and 12″ to the right, and mark those lines. Measure up 1¾″ from the bottom of the canvas,

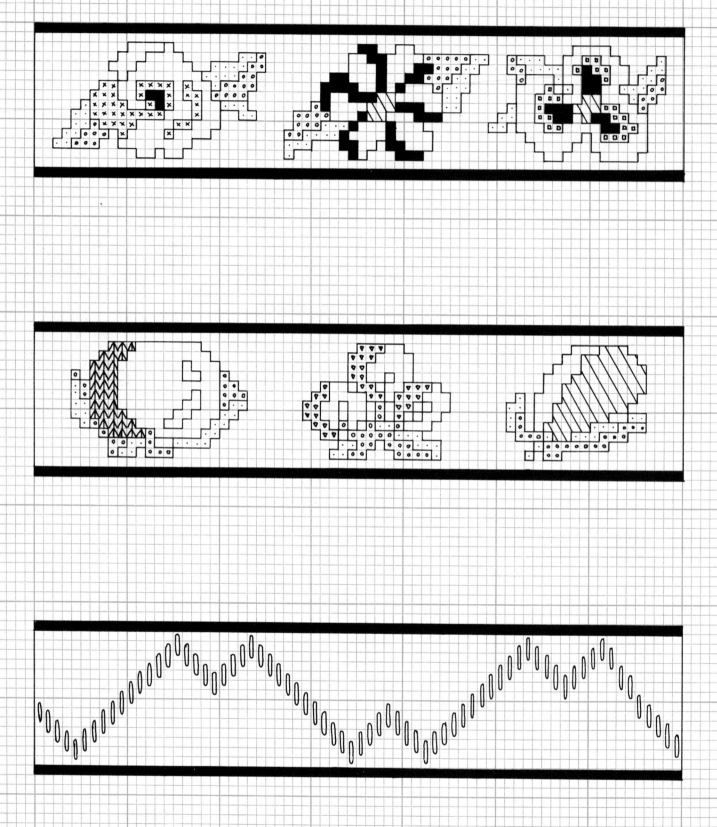

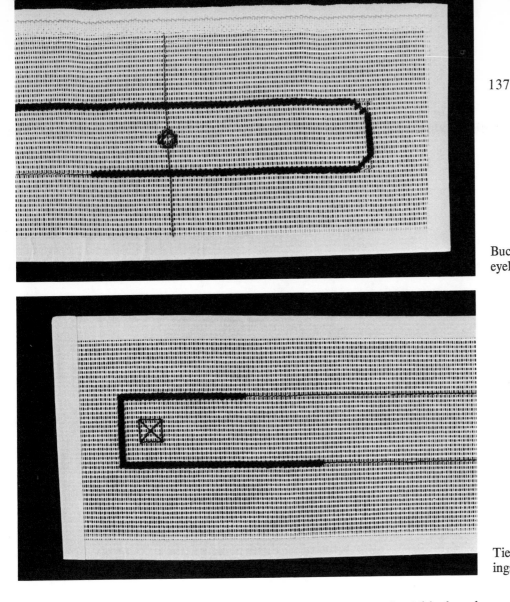

Buckle belt: Placement of center eyelet

Tie belt: Placement of tie openings

and mark that line all the way across. Now mark across on the 16th thread above, or whatever number you need. These are the guidelines for the width of the belt. Now stitch one row all the way around on the guidelines.

Next you should make square openings for the ties to go through. The photo of the layout for the tie belt shows where they should be cut—½″ in from each end. Mark a square 6 x 6 stitches on each side; make sure the square falls in the center of the belt. Cut in 2 diagonal lines going from corner to corner inside the square. Fold back the four little tabs of canvas and, using double yarn, stitch around the square, making sure to put a stitch in each hole of the canvas. This is finishing clean (page 45) in miniature.

Now that the tie openings are finished, you can fill in your pattern on the belt. If you want to use a name or initials, lay the letters out on graph paper, and stitch them so the center of the monogram or name is on the center back of the belt. Get the top and bottom guidelines for the letters from one of the alphabet graphs. Now you can fill in the balance of the belt with any pattern you wish.

Graphed designs for belts:
16 threads wide

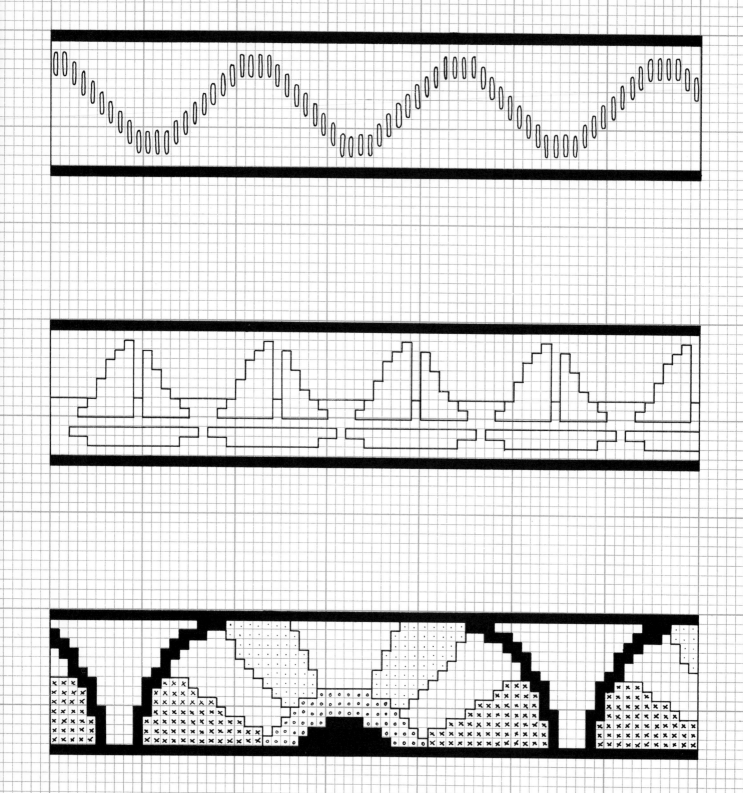

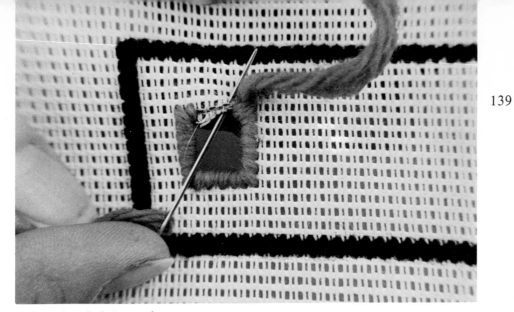

Reinforcing tie-belt opening

FINISHING CLEAN AND BLOCKING

Now that the belt is finished, the edges should be finished clean. Block the canvas first (page 43). For either style of belt, trim the canvas and finish the edges following the directions on page 45.

FINISH FOR BUCKLE BELT

Back the belt with felt, ribbon, or leather, according to the directions on page 47.

If you are using a harness buckle rather than a square buckle, you will need a belt loop to hold the flap of the belt in place once the belt is buckled. Cut a strip of canvas 4½″ long by 8 double threads wide. Fold it in half lengthwise. Using double yarn, go along one edge using the clean-finish technique, then turn the strip around and finish the other side. Press it flat, then join the two ends together. Slip it around the belt. (A fancier, lined loop made like a tiny belt is shown in the next photo.)

Now put the buckle on. Poke a small hole in the center of the buckle line for the prong of the buckle to go through. Then bend back the 1½″ flap, and stitch it down by hand (catching the belt loop under it) so that the buckle is held securely in place. At the other end, the eyelets should be put in 1″ apart. Put in the center eyelet first, 4¼″ from the end, and then two more on each side.

FINISH FOR TIE BELT

Use felt, ribbon, or leather, and follow the directions given on page 47. You should glue the backing on first, and then cut out the tie holes. Put the ties through the holes and the belt is ready to be worn.

Graphed designs for belts:
15 threads wide

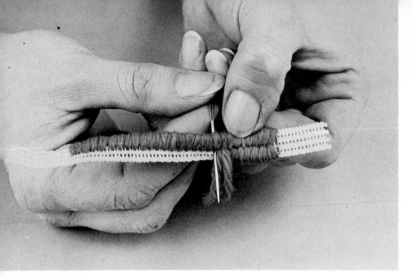

Making simple loop for buckle belt

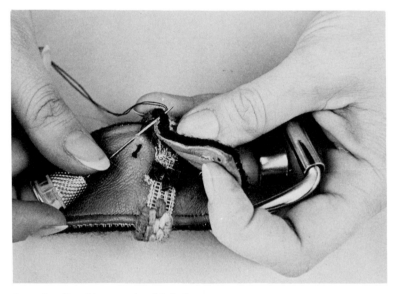

Securing lined loop on buckle belt

Looping tie onto tie belt

Hats

MATERIALS

(Color picture 16)

Penelope canvas, 22″ x 17″ (10/in. or 5/in.). Cut your canvas the same size, whichever mesh you use; just make sure you follow the graph for the correct mesh size.

A piece of felt or fabric to line the hat (this should be 22″ x 17″ also)

Ribbon ties (1 yard), or enough extra yarn to crochet or braid the ties

Masking tape

Yarns, needle, thimble, scissors

1. Lay out the hat on the canvas by following the layout for the canvas mesh size you have chosen. The 5/in. will work up faster, but the 10/in. will give you more detail. Fill in the entire pattern for the hat, using the dotted center lines as guidelines. Outline the hat first, and then fill in the pattern.

2. Block the finished canvas back to its original shape (page 43).

3. Now trim away some of the canvas from the back seams. Leave about ½″ to 1″ seam allowance on each side.

4. Next you join the two back seams. Using double yarn, come up through the first hole at the top of the seam and go into the corresponding hole on the other side of the seam. (See "Joining Seams," page 46). Join the seam all the way to the bottom and secure the yarn by running it through the finished work on the back. Close the other seam the same way. Press the seams open.

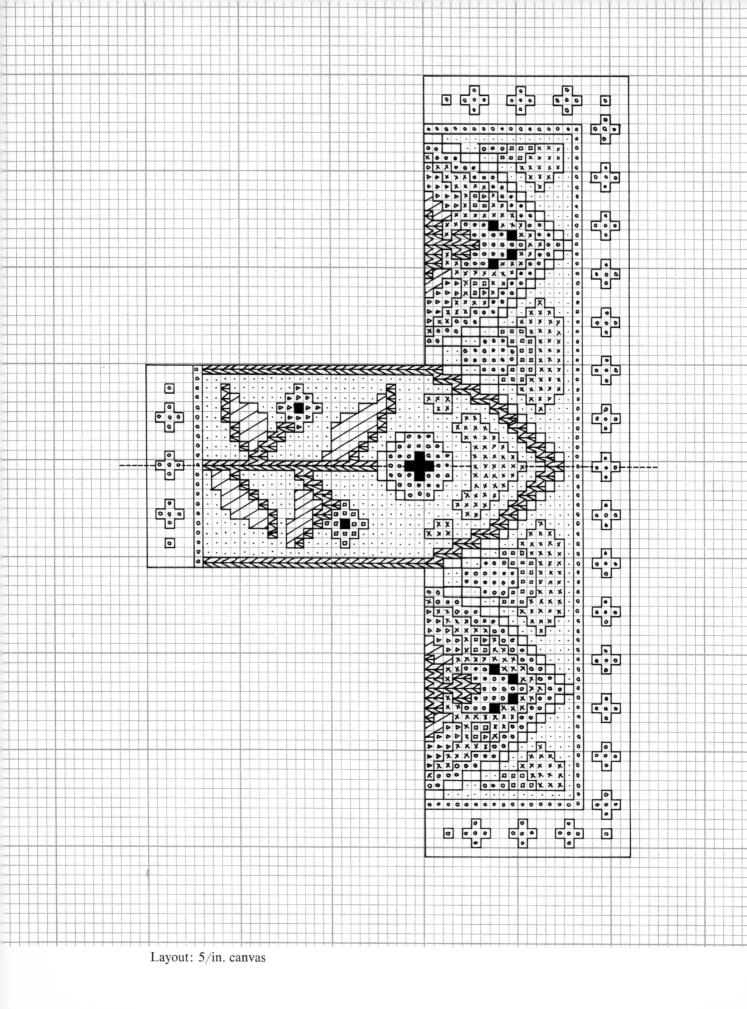

Layout: 5/in. canvas

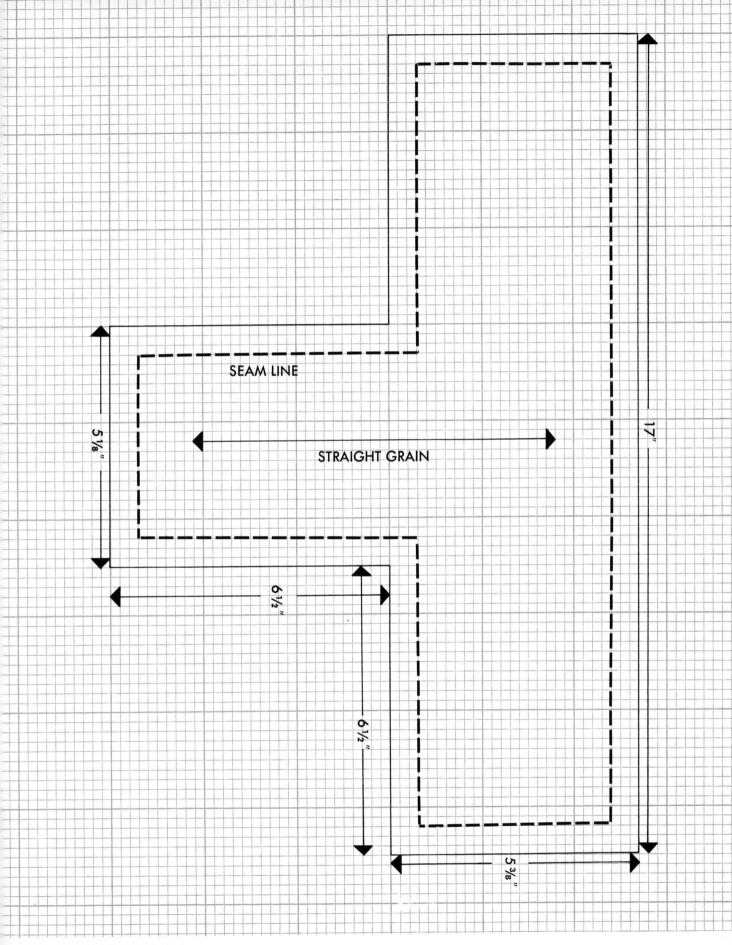

SEAM LINE

STRAIGHT GRAIN

5 1/8"

17"

6 1/2"

6 1/2"

5 3/8"

Layout: 10/in. canvas

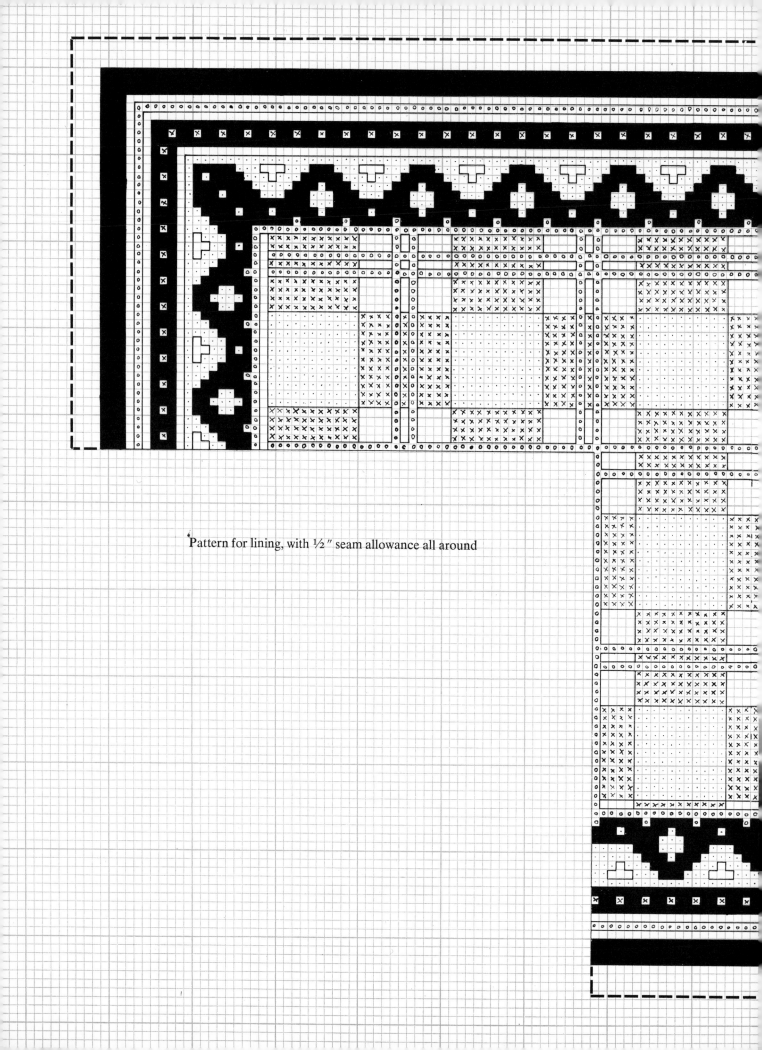

Pattern for lining, with ½″ seam allowance all around

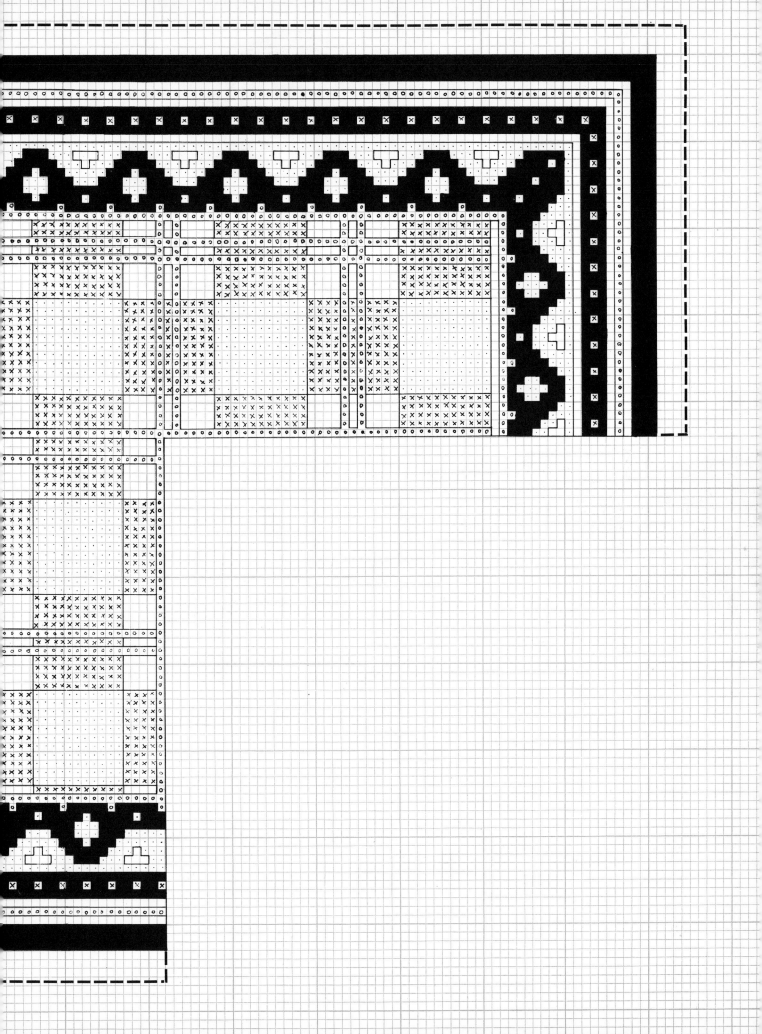

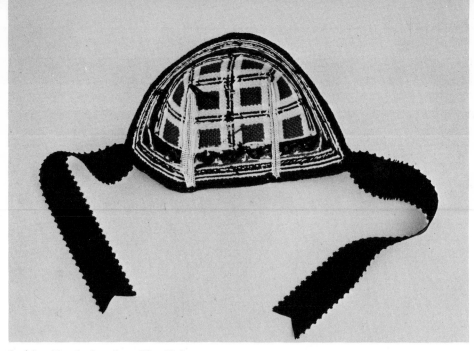

146

Inside of hat before installing lining

Sew on ribbons before putting in lining.

Pin lining securely before tacking in place.

5. Now finish the edges clean all around. Follow the directions on page 45. Trim the canvas between the third and fourth threads away from the needlepoint, and remember to use double yarn.

6. Make your ties out of yarn or attach ribbons at the front corners of the hat. Each tie should be about 13″ long. Sew them by hand inside the front corners.

7. Then make the lining. Cut out a piece of fabric following the pattern given, and join the two back seams by machine, or by hand with very small running stitches. Press the seams open.

Place the lining inside the hat, matching up the two back seams with the back seams of the needlepoint. Tack the hat seams and lining seams together. Turn the lining in ½″ all around the edges, and pin it to the hat. Now slip-stitch it all around by hand. If you use felt, you do not have to turn the edges in because the felt will not fray; trim away any excess instead. Now press with an iron around the inside edges of the lining.

Patchwork pillow, 10/in. canvas, page 157

Covered Boxes

MATERIALS

(Color pictures 17 & 18)

Plain, unfinished wooden box. The box should have flat sides and square corners and there should be a lip inside the lid. You can usually find these in various sizes at a handcraft or department* store.

A set of small hinges to attach the lid and box once they have been covered with needlepoint.

Penelope canvas (10/in.). You need two pieces of canvas, one for the lid and one for the bottom of the box. Take the measurement in square inches of the top of the lid, to this add the depth of the lid on all four sides, then allow another 2″ of canvas all around. For the bottom of the box, the measurement of the bottom base is the same as the top of the lid. To this add the depth of the side of the box on all four sides, then allow another 2″ of canvas all around.

Elmer's glue and a small flat paintbrush

Pushpins (½″ long), 2 dozen or more to secure needlepoint to box once it's glued down

Staple gun to attach canvas to bottom of box

Piece of felt to glue onto the bottom

Patchwork pillow, 5/in. canvas, page 157

* Write to the O-P Craft Company, Inc., Sandusky, Ohio 44870, to order boxes.

Graph paper, 10 squares per inch—two pieces large enough for the lid top plus its sides and for the bottom base plus the sides of the box

Optional: If you want the inside of the box to be painted or covered with fabric, you should do this before the needlepoint is applied. Use spray paint and let it dry thoroughly. If you want to use fabric, it should be a piece of lightweight cotton or something comparable. It should be applied with Elmer's glue; use the same technique of glueing to a hard surface (page 49) as for applying needlepoint.

1. Cut your two pieces of canvas according to the directions given in the list of materials. Remember it *must* be penelope canvas. Bind the edges with masking tape.

2. You should have accurate measurements for this project, so lay it out on the graph paper. Mark out the lid-top measurement first, then add on the four sides of the lid. The lid-top and bottom-base measurements are the same, so draw them again on the other piece of graph paper, and on each side add the measurements of the sides of the box. The example illustrated is a box 4⅞″ x 4⅞″, with lid sides 1¼″ deep and the sides of the box 2¾″ deep. It is laid out on the *canvas* like this:

3. Now you can plan your design on the graph paper. If you want to center a design in any of the areas, count the total number of spaces for the area, both across and up and down, and divide them by two. For the sides of the lid and of the box, lay out your designs to within *2 rows of the box edges* (the dotted lines on the illustrated layout mark the rows at which you should stop stitching) and to the solid lines at the corners (which will later be joined). You do not need any needlepoint on the bottom base, as this will be covered with felt.

Remember when laying out your patterns to place each one so that it will be right side up on each side of the box. (The lettering on each panel in the illustration is turned in the right direction.) Also, when filling in your pattern, have your stitches going in the correct direction in each section. This is indicated in the illustrations with the two black stitches drawn in each section.

4. Start with the bottom of the box and fill in one row of stitches on the canvas all around the bottom measurement. (This is marked with a solid black line on the layout.) The one row of stitches will be sufficient to cover the bottom edges of the box. Now fill in the sides of the box, following your graph, completing them to within 2 rows of the top edges (dotted lines) and to the solid lines at all four corners.

Now, for the top of the box, fill in all the design, again completing the pattern to the solid lines at the corners and to within 2 rows of the outside edges.

5. Block both pieces of canvas (page 43) and let them dry thoroughly so that they can then be trimmed, finished clean, and applied to the box.

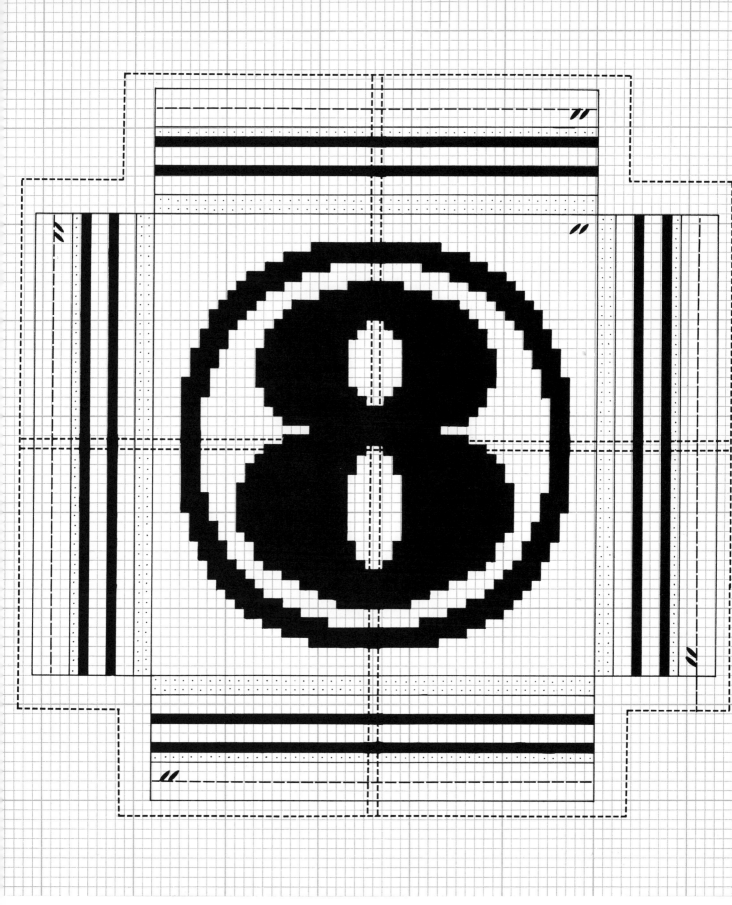

Layout of top of box

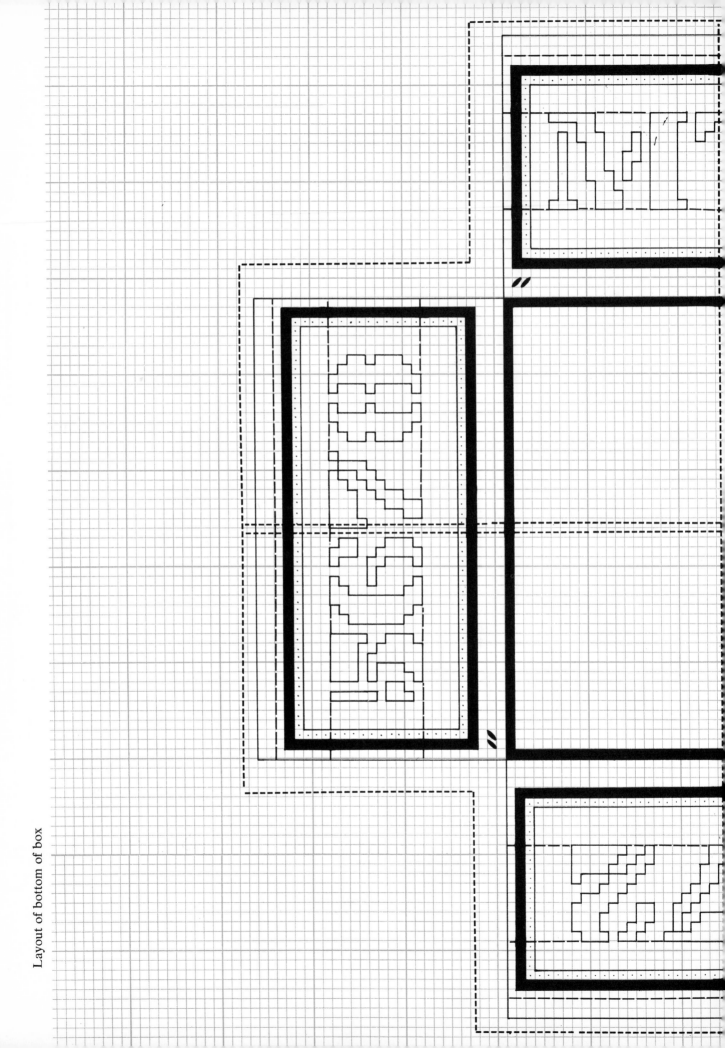

Layout of bottom of box

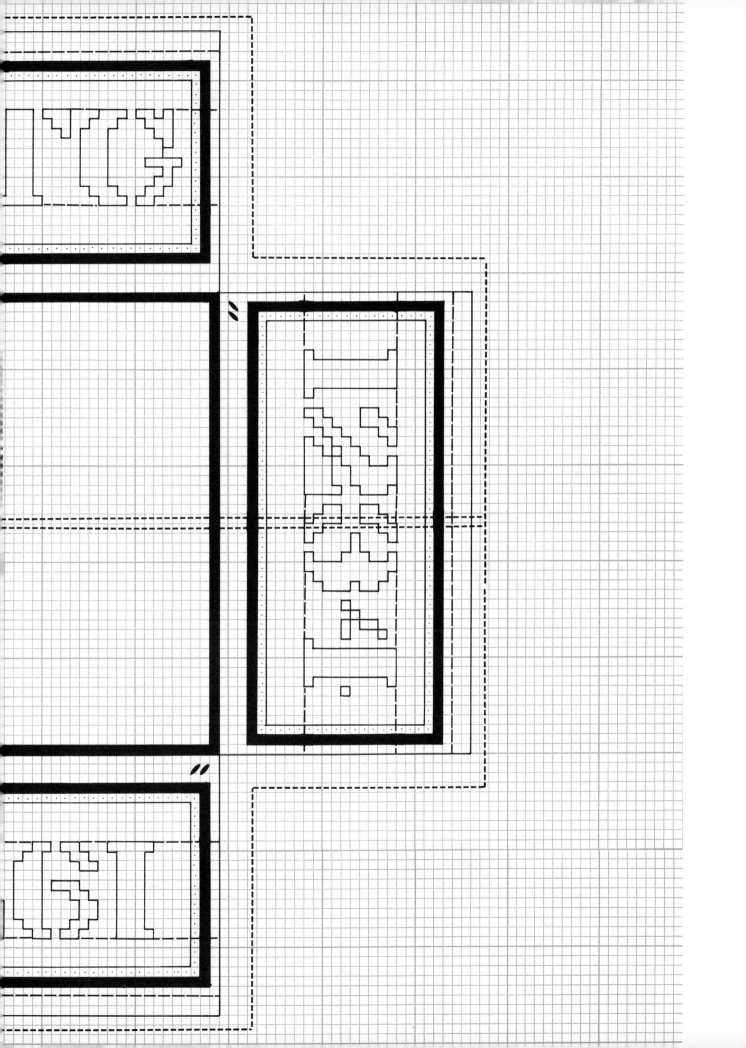

On both the bottom and lid, cut away excess canvas beyond the stitching. Finish edges clean.

Snip canvas in the corners so seams will fold in flat.

6. Cut out all the corners and the edges between the third and fourth threads beyond the stitching. (You can cut between the fourth and fifth lines in the corners, if you want, to make the corner seams easier to handle.) Now you are ready to finish the edges clean on the sides of both the lid and the bottom. (The corners will be joined later.) See page 45 for finishing clean. Then, snip the canvas in the corners so that the "seam allowances" will fold in flat.

7. Put some Elmer's glue in a small container. Add a few drops of water so that it is of a consistency to spread easily with a brush. Now brush only the top of the box with glue. Place the lid top of the needlepoint on the glued surface, making sure to line it up evenly. Now brush glue on the sides of the lid. Secure the needlepoint all along the edges of the lid with pushpins, folding in the raw edges of canvas at each corner as you go.

Now, using double yarn, join the corners. (In the photographs, this is shown being done on the *bottom* of the box.) Turn the lid upside down. Pull the yarn through the bottom hole of the seam from the inside, and tuck the loose ends inside with your needle. Stitch over the seam, lining up the canvas holes on each side. When you get to the top of the corner, put your needle down the seam, pull the yarn through, and snip it off closely.

Leave in the pushpins until the glue is dry. If some of the edges do not stay glued, use a toothpick to spread more glue under them, and secure once again with pushpins.

8. Turn the bottom of the box upside down. Spread the bottom base with glue, and place the unstitched center of the needlepoint on it, making sure you line up all the edges. With a staple gun, go all around the edges of the base just inside the finished needlepoint. Turn the box right side up, and spread glue on the sides. Fold in the raw edges of canvas at each corner.

Secure the top edges to the box with pushpins. Using double yarn, join the corners together, working from bottom to top. Leave in the pushpins until the glue is dry.

9. Now the box is complete except for the finishing touches. Cut a piece of felt to fit, and glue it to the bottom base. To put on the hinges: Place the lid on the box and tie a string around it, as you would tie a package, to hold the two pieces together and properly lined up. Now open the hinges, place them on the back of the box, and screw each one in right through the needlepoint.

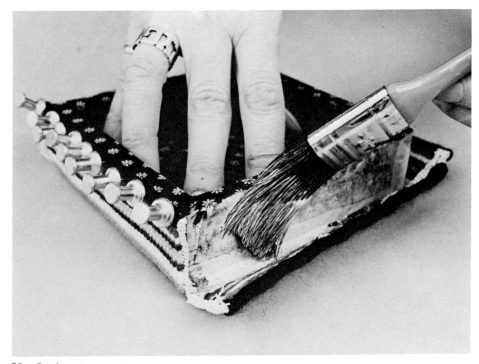

Use flat brush to apply glue. Fold in seams at corners.

Tack all along the edges with pushpins.

On bottom of box, secure canvas with staple gun inside needlepoint.

To finish, put needle down the seam, pull yarn through, snip off closely.

Stitch over seam, lining up holes.

Tie strings around the box to line up top and bottom. Screw on hinges right through needlepoint.

Patchwork Pillows

(Color pictures 19 & 20)

Everything ever written in English (and not just English!)—including great ideas, philosophies, plays, novels, doctrines, histories, and recipes—has been constructed using combinations selected from only 26 letters. Now it's your turn to create a one-of-a-kind combination, a patchwork pillow using letters, designs, and colors selected from (but not necessarily limited to) the patterns shown here. The odds against anyone's duplicating your arrangement are astronomical, even if you don't add a single design of your own in any of the blocks.

You can make a pillow that will finish approximately 13″ x 13″, or one that will be 17″ x 17″ finished, depending on which canvas mesh size you work with. A layout for each size is shown. There are eight blocks of patterns. Choose your letters from the Shadow Gothic Boxed alphabet (page 61). Start arranging and decide what combination you would like to make.

MATERIALS

Canvas, 10/in., cut 18″ x 18″—or 5/in., cut 22″ x 22″. These dimensions allow for about 2½″ of extra canvas around your finished pattern.

Yarns. Use 3-strand Persian wool for 10/in. canvas, or bulky rug yarn for the 5/in.

Waterproof marking pen

Masking tape

Needle, thimble, scissors

1. Cut the piece of canvas and bind the edges with masking tape. 157

2. Fold canvas in half vertically. Mark the vertical line on the fold. Now fold the canvas in half horizontally, and mark that line on the fold. If you use 5/in. canvas, the total count on the design is 86 lines, an even number. Therefore, there have to be *two* center lines, both horizontally and vertically. If you use 10/in. canvas, the total count on the design is 137, an odd number; therefore, there is only one center line each way.

3. The point at which the lines cross marks the center of the design; use this as your point of reference to begin laying out the blocks on the canvas. On 5/in. canvas, start by marking out the little center motif where the borders between blocks cross. On 10/in. canvas, start by marking out the center block. Then count out the positions of all the blocks and of the borders between them by reading the printed layout, using the crossed center lines as reference from which to count in all four directions. (Instructions for most of the projects in this book tell you always to lay out designs this way, starting from the center, never the corner, of a design. This is not only so that your design will be centered on the canvas, but also to make it easier to count out the four corners of the design so that they come out even.)

4. Now decide which design you would like to put in each block. The possible combinations are endless, so you can experiment on paper with many different assortments until you decide what you like best. Each of the patterns and letters will fit into each block. On the 5/in. canvas, you can do four different ones or make them all the same, or combine blocks of patterns and letters, or use all letters. Each pattern is two colors, and they can all be the same two colors, as in the picture of the black-and-white 10/in. pillow (page 147); or each one can be a different pair of colors, as in the 5/in. pillow (page 148). Stitch each block completely, one at a time. If you're not sure exactly what color combinations you want to use, start with one you like best and once you've completed that, it may inspire you for the others.

5. When you have all the blocks filled in with patterns, fill in the borders between the blocks and all around the edge of the design, following either the 5/in. or 10/in. layout.

6. Now block and back the needlepoint (page 43 and page 49). You can have just as much fun with the pillow backing as you've had with the patterns on the front. Try making a patchwork back, using fabric swatches sewn together. Or shop around in fabric departments for a print that will complement the design you have made. Or choose one of the bright colors from your pattern and make the back a solid color; felt is usually a good fabric to use, because it comes in a variety of colors and is easy to work with.

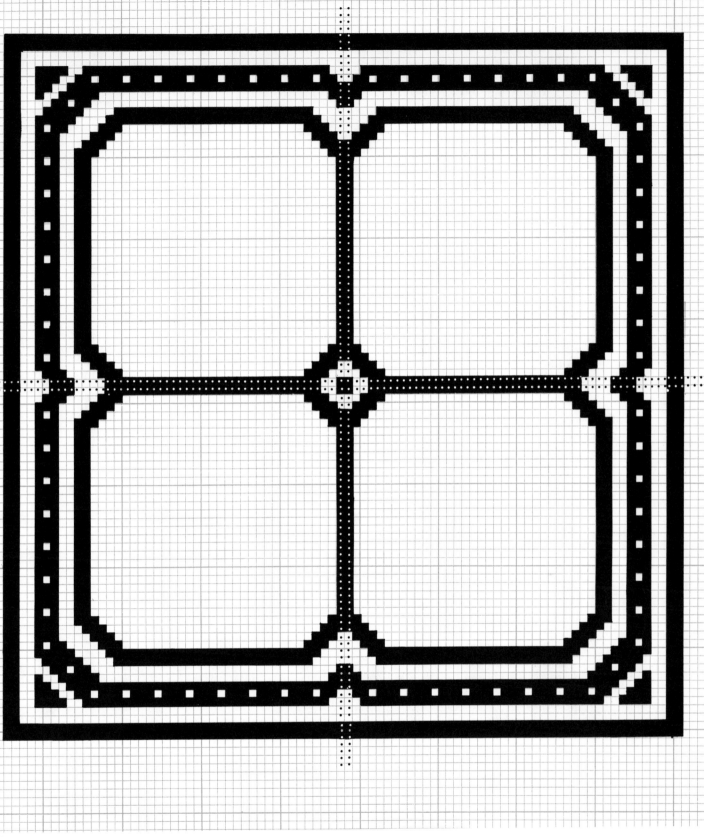

Layout for 4-patch pillow

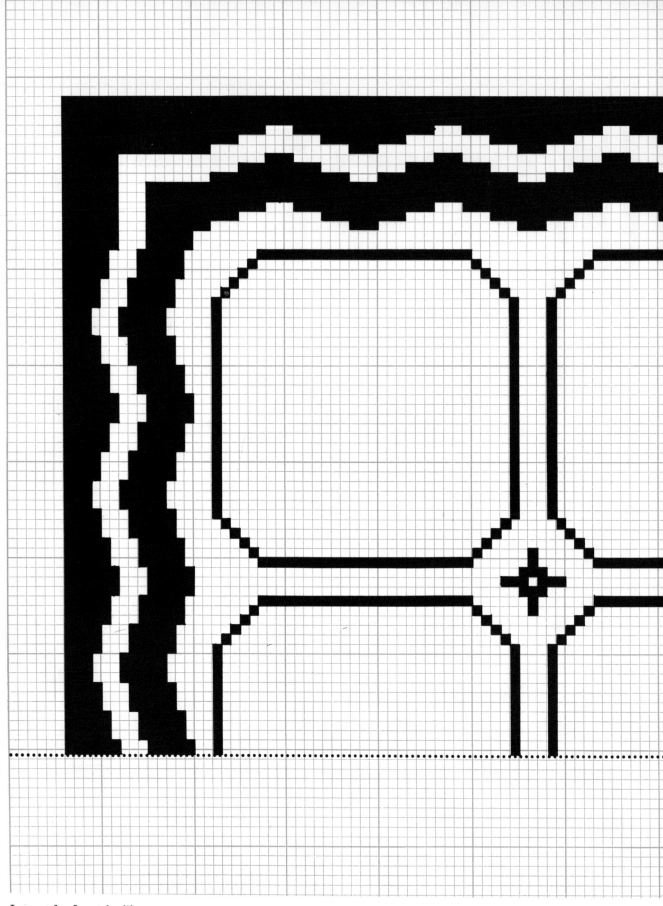

Layout for 9-patch pillow

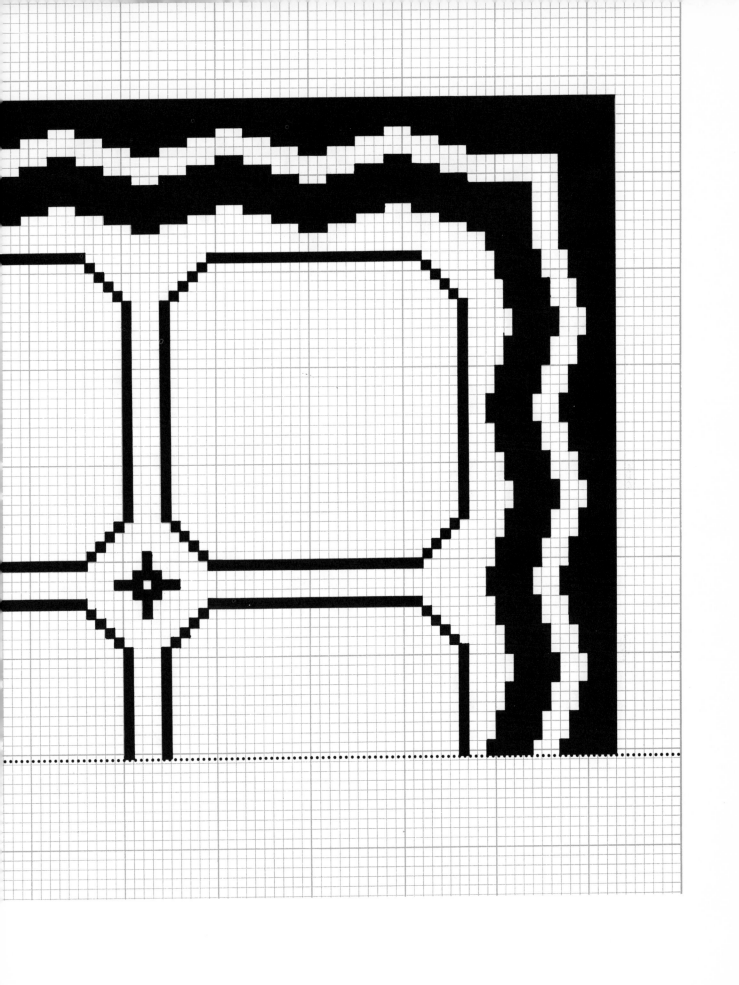

Patterns for pillow patches

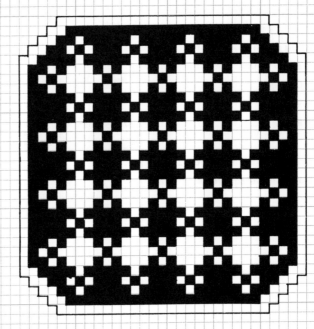

166   Graph paper, 10 squares per inch, if you wish to lay out your own design

Yarns, needle, thimble, scissors

1. Cut your canvas and bind the edges with masking tape.
2. Find your crossing center lines by folding the canvas both vertically and horizontally and marking the fold lines. Use these as your guidelines to copy the graphed layout for the checkerboard or for your own design. Copy the half of the checkerboard shown in the graph once on the right-hand side of the canvas, then repeat exactly on the left; the colors will line up across the checkerboard as shown in the color picture on page 173. If you want the piece larger, you can leave the blocks the same size, but add a wider border by continuing the border stripes farther out all the way around.
3. Stitch to within 2 rows of the finished measurement that you want. If you are following the layout given, stitch the border to the dotted line, which will leave the last 2 rows unstitched.
4. Now block your canvas (page 43), making sure to get it square.
5. Finish the edge clean all around (page 45). Use double black yarn, or whatever color you wish, to finish the edges. Place the needlepoint on the tabletop. You can glue it to the table surface if you want it to be permanent (page 49). Now put the glass on top, and have fun playing.

Place Mats or Centerpiece

By changing your measurements, you really might use the same principle for place mats, covering each one with a separate piece of glass. (The edges of the glass should be very carefully sanded.) Better, a needlepoint mat, with or without glass, could be used as a centerpiece for a large table.

Photo Album
or
Book Cover

MATERIALS

(Color picture 22)

Canvas (10/in.), cut 30″ x 17″

Three-ring loose-leaf binder, measuring 10⅝″ x 11⅝″, with a 2″-wide spine. My layout is made for this size, but adjustments can be made on the layout for any other size.

Acetate-covered pages to put inside the binder if you do want to use it for a photo album

Yarns. Use 3-strand Persian wool, or any that will cover 10/in. canvas.

Waterproof marking pen

Masking tape

Felt or leather, about ½ yard, to use for the inside of the book cover

Elmer's glue slightly thinned with water and 1 can of spray glue

A flat brush 1″ wide to apply glue

Hand staple gun with ¼″ staples

Graph paper, 10 squares per inch

Needle, thimble, scissors

167

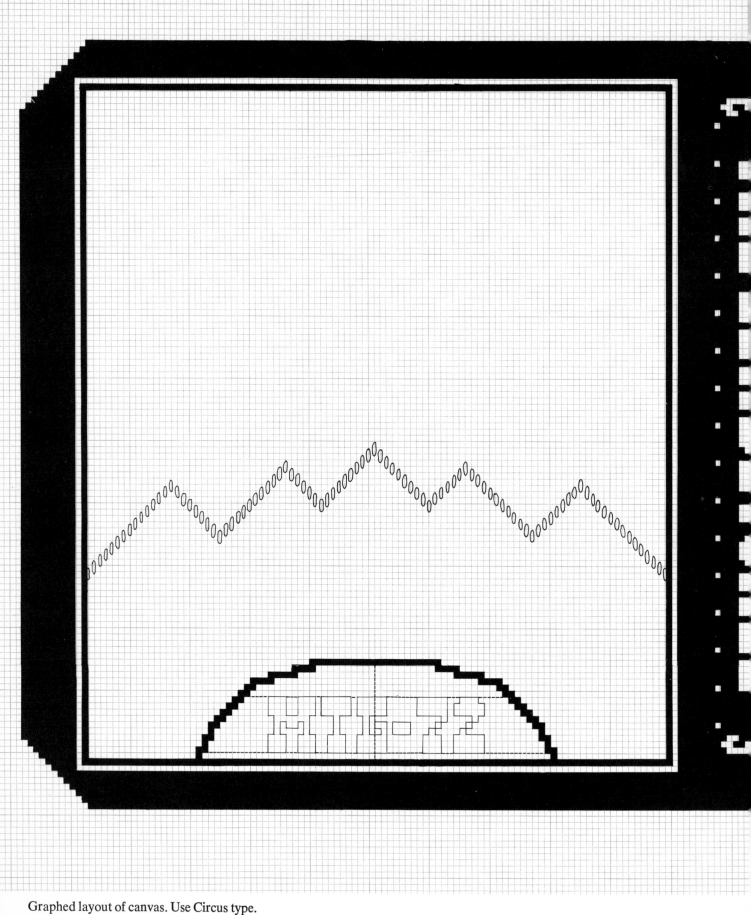

Graphed layout of canvas. Use Circus type.

PICTURE
BOOK

1. Cut the piece of canvas and bind the edges with masking tape. The 17″ measurement is the straight grain of the canvas (parallel to the selvage edge).

2. Fold the canvas in half vertically and mark the vertical fold line. This is the guideline for the center of the book spine and is marked with a vertical dotted line on the layout. Fold the canvas in half horizontally and mark the center of the vertical line. Put your name, or whatever else you want, on the spine: Using the Circus type (page 58), lay out the letters on graph paper and center the word or words using the horizontal dotted line on the graph as your center guideline.

3. Next stitch in the black outline around the front and back covers. Make sure you count accurately, because these are your most important guidelines.

4. Fill in the front cover. The areas of color are broken down in the layout and you can see as many or as few as you wish. If you want to change the words PICTURE BOOK to something else, lay out your words on graph paper and center them, using the dotted lines on the layout as a guide. Use the Circus type if that is what you used on the spine.

5. Fill in the back cover. Put your initials and date in first. If you want to make a longer signature, allow more stitches in the center of the arch shape that outlines it. Do one row of the bargello stitch following the layout and continue this stitch until the entire back cover is filled in. Use as many or as few colors as you want.

6. Now fill in all the background on the spine and the front and back covers with black, as it is on the layout.

7. Now block your canvas, making sure you square it out accurately. Once it is completely dry and squared out, trim the excess canvas, leaving about ½″ of raw canvas beyond the last row of needlepoint.

8. Lay the finished needlepoint right side down on a flat surface. Now take the book cover and, using a 1″ flat brush and Elmer's glue watered down, spread glue over the entire outside of the cover, front and back. Let the glue dry for a minute or until it is tacky to the touch. Open the cover and place it on the finished needlepoint, making sure you line up the edges.

9. Now the edges of the needlepoint must be turned to the inside of the cover. With the brush, spread glue around the inside edges of the cover. Bend the needlepoint in and pin into place. Put pins in at an angle, about 1″ apart all around. Slip the needlepoint under the binder on the spine. Once it is all pinned, use a staple gun to hold it permanently all around, and take the pins out.

"Paint" the back of the loose-leaf binder with glue.

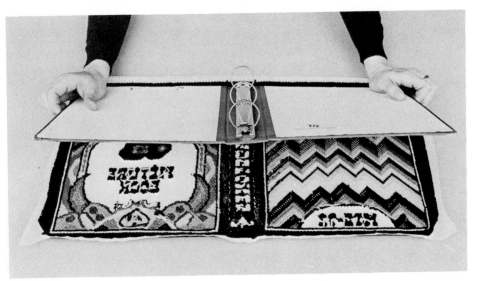

Line up open binder and needle-point carefully.

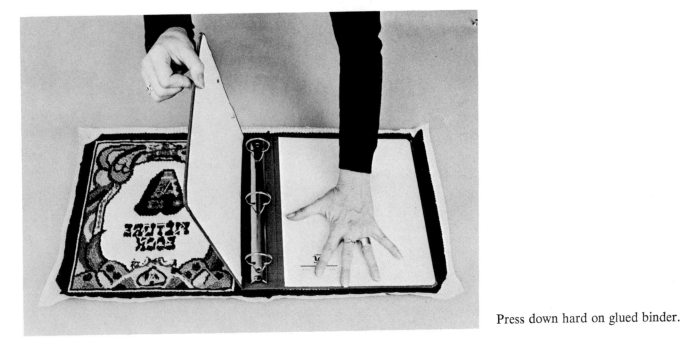

Press down hard on glued binder.

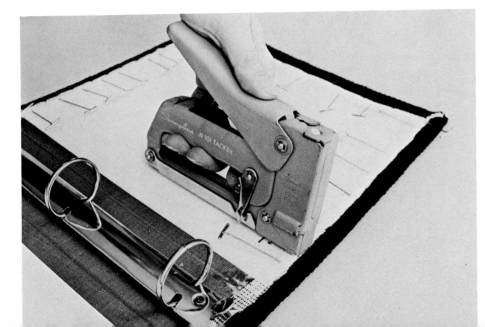

Once needlepoint edges have been turned in, glued, and pinned, staple around edges to secure permanently.

172   10. The corners should now be stitched together. Starting at the outside edge, bring the yarn up from underneath and stitch down.

11. Now measure the inside panel and cut 2 pieces of felt or leather to finish the inside. Spray the back of the felt or leather with adhesive and place it inside the book.

Fill your pages with snapshots and place the album where everyone can enjoy your work and your pictures.

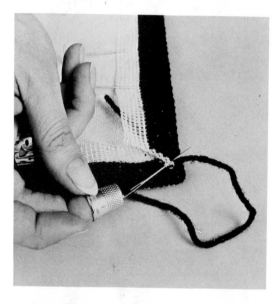

Stitch corners together, working from the outside in.

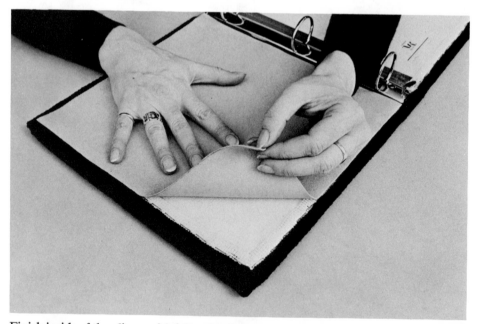

Finish inside of the album with felt or leather.

Opposite: Game-table top, page 165

Next page: Photo album, page 167

Giant Foulard Pattern Rug

MATERIALS

(Color picture 23)

Penelope canvas (5/in.), 39/40" width. You need a length of canvas 55" for a rug that will be approximately 3' x 4½' finished. You cannot make it wider unless you piece the canvas, but it can be longer if you want. Each square is 15" x 15", so add 15" for each square in addition to those on the layout.

Heavy wool or acrylic yarn. Make sure it covers the canvas.

Waterproof marking pen

Needle, thimble, scissors

Rug binding tape (1½" to 2" wide) for the edges—about 6 yards for the size given, more if you make the rug longer

1. Cut your canvas and bind the ends with masking tape. You do not have to bind the sides because you are using the full width of the canvas, which is finished with selvage edges.

2. Fold the canvas in half lengthwise and mark the thread on the fold line. This is the black center line that separates the 2 rows of squares and is your guideline for the layout. Outline each of the 6 squares with black or whatever other color you wish to use. Make sure you follow the layout and count accurately. Once the outlines of all the squares are stitched in, stitch in the black diamond-shaped motif in each one. Now stitch the yellow inner border of each square and the two-tone centers of each diamond motif. Fill in the background of each square, then add your outside striped border all around.

Graph of one square of foulard pattern. Rug consists of 6 squares plus continuous border on 5/in. canvas. Dotted line indicates the center of the rug lengthwise.

180 NOTE: I suggest you use the basketweave and continental stitches for this project so that the back will be padded and durable.

3. You need a large area to block the rug. If you do it yourself, you might try blocking it on the floor over another rug. Pin it down, press, using a wet cloth, and let it dry (page 43).

4. The rug binding tape is 1½″ to 2″ wide, so trim your canvas so that the binding tape will cover the raw canvas when the canvas is folded under.

5. Sew on the rug binding by hand at the edge of the finished needlepoint. Now turn back both the binding tape and the excess canvas under it, and press flat. Hem the tape down by hand and miter the corners so that they are square and lie flat. Then press the binding all around again.

Sewing seam binding on rug

INDEX

ABOUT THE AUTHORS

MEREDITH GLADSTONE was graduated from The Rhode Island School of Design and is a successful designer of junior sportswear and of modern needlepoint kits distributed nationally by Columbia-Minerva. Her work has been featured in many major publications. GARY GLADSTONE is a photographer and graphic designer. His work has been published in *Life, The Saturday Evening Post, McCall's, Seventeen, Harper's Bazaar,* and *Sports Illustrated,* and he is the author of *Hey, Hey, Can't Catch Me!,* a book about children in words and color photographs. The Gladstones live in New York City.